Research Techniques
for Scholars and Students
in Religion and Theology

Research Techniques
for Scholars and Students
in Religion and Theology

Dennis C. Tucker

 Information Today, Inc.

Medford, New Jersey

Second printing, 2002

Research Techniques for Scholars and Students in Religion and Theology

Copyright © 2000 by Dennis C. Tucker

Library of Congress Cataloging-in-Publication Data

Tucker, Dennis C.
    Research techniques for scholars and students in religion and theology / by Dennis C. Tucker.
      cm.
    Includes bibliographical references and index.
    ISBN 1-57387-089-7
    1. Religion—Research. 2. Theology—Research.   I. Title.

    BL41 .T83 1999

                          99-053871

Printed and bound in the United States of America

Publisher: Thomas H. Hogan, Sr.
Editor-in-Chief: John B. Bryans
Managing Editor: Janet M. Spavlik
Production Manager: M. Heide Dengler
Book Designers: Patricia F. Kirkbride
                Jeremy M. Pellegrin
Cover Designer: Jeremy M. Pellegrin
Indexer: Laurie Andriot

Table of Contents

Introduction

A wise person once said, "Give a man a fish and you feed him for a day; teach him to fish and you feed him for a lifetime."

Educators have often been told that we teach people, not subjects. Yet, if we teach a person a subject, we still have not fulfilled our mission. We must teach him or her how to learn more about that subject without assistance from us. He or she needs to progress beyond the limit of our knowledge; therefore, a good foundation in research skills is an essential part of a good education and one that will last a lifetime.

Years of experience both in teaching and in library work have shown us that we educators have often failed in teaching research skills. It is the purpose of this book to provide instruction in the basic skills necessary for doing research in the area of religion and theology. We are going to look at libraries and how they can be used to the best advantage. We will attempt to offer some basic resources and techniques that can be used by the student of religion while in school, and by the graduate—the professional, the pastor, the youthworker, the missionary—who no longer has access to a teacher or faculty member for direction but must gather information independently.

We will discuss, explain, and demonstrate six major components essential to the responsible development of information retrieval and utilization skills in the field of religion and theology. The order of discussion is as follows:

FIRST, we will look at the overall layout of the library itself (whether at a college, university, or public library). We will discuss the organization of the holdings and their various categories and functions. We will list and explain the various staff positions typical in a library, and we will make some references to general policies of utilization commonly found in libraries.

SECOND, we will examine the library catalog, and its smaller unit, the catalog record. Each record contains a wealth of information that many nonlibrarians don't even know exists and that can serve as a springboard to a vast pool of other resources.

THIRD, we will consider the reference collection and briefly discuss what distinguishes a reference book from a nonreference book. At the same time, we will outline some basic criteria for evaluating a reference work and look at some of the major reference sources in the subject area of religion and theology.

FOURTH, the professional who wishes to keep current in his or her field must know how to use the periodical literature to locate the latest research. We will look at periodicals and their indexes—both the traditional manual indexes and their newer counterparts, automated indexes.

FIFTH, we'll look at the Internet, the World Wide Web, and other electronic resources. We'll look at some criteria for evaluating them, examining the various types of resources, and see how they compare.

FINALLY, we will briefly discuss and illustrate an effective method of research documentation and discuss ways of developing a research paper from the choice of the initial topic to its completion.

We will take a look at the most valuable library resource of all—the library staff, and especially the reference librarian. This information professional is a trained researcher with skills that will allow him or her to locate information in any field, be it theology, philosophy, medicine, law, or engineering. Nowadays, the well-prepared reference librarian is not only a researcher, but also an expert in logic (Boolean, to be precise), information management, and computer systems.

When I began graduate school, I experienced an overwhelming feeling of awe every time I entered the library—so much knowledge contained therein and I would only be able to begin to scratch the surface. As time went by, I came to the conclusion that only a small percentage of that volume was fresh knowledge, and the rest was repetition. As I developed my research skills, my final conclusion was that, although I could never learn it all, with the proper tools, I could find any single piece or pieces of information that I wanted; the rest didn't interest me anyway. In short, my research ability allowed me to separate the valuable from the less valuable and the valueless. It is the hope of author and publisher that this work will help the beginning researcher develop the same skills.

Author's note: At the risk of appearing insensitive to gender-neutral language issues, in most cases we have chosen to use masculine references as "gender generic" rather than the cumbersome he/she, him/her, etc. When all is said and done, a book reads more smoothly written the old-fashioned way.

Chapter One

The Library as a Physical Space

One of the first things the researcher will want to do when beginning research is to find a library, whether it be an academic or a public library. Once you have located the library, we suggest a visit just to have a look around. Just browse to get a general idea of the layout. Locate the various stack areas and the different types of collections that are contained within the building. Find the bathrooms and water fountains and the quiet areas for study. Perhaps now is a good time to locate a favorite hideaway that will later become your special secret place for studying.

Some libraries will have printed brochures that give information on the library, telling about its various collections, special display areas, where the various parts of the collection are located, etc. If such a brochure is not readily visible, ask the library staff if one is available.

Other libraries are even more elaborate in orienting new users to the library. An increasing number of libraries are using audio or videocassettes for orientation. It is sometimes possible to check out a videotape for home use. Other times the library may have a special viewing area where you can go to watch the tape that is, in essence, a guided tour of the building and its collections. Some libraries have audiotapes that you can borrow along with a cassette player for in-house use. These tapes contain a self-guided tour of the library. You play the tape and follow its directions for a walking tour of the building.

Some libraries may have personnel who will give a guided tour of the building. Depending upon the policy of the library, a tour may be available at any time upon request or only at scheduled times, in which case you can sign up to come back later and join a group. Most colleges and universities have some type of library tour (often called "bibliographic instruction tour").

The introductory visit to the library is a good time to acquaint yourself with its particular policies and procedures. What types of materials can be checked out? For how long? How do you get a library card? What types of materials must be used in house? What are the library hours? Is there an after-hours study area? What is the availability of special collections, interlibrary loan, and computer databases? The more the researcher knows about the building and its layout, the more comfortable he or she will feel using its services and dealing with its personnel.

A good library contains more than just books. It will have a variety of educational materials, aids, and services with a staff of professionally trained individuals happy to assist the inquiring researcher who is seeking to utilize its resources. There is a logic to the arrangement of these materials and the organization of the various functions of the staff. The serious researcher needs to acquaint him or herself with the library and its methods, concepts, and procedures.

At this point, it will be helpful to point out the fundamental structure of the holdings and the staff positions of the typical library. Just as not everyone who works in a doctor's office is a doctor, neither is everyone who works in a library a librarian. Just as you would not expect the doctor's receptionist to perform surgery, you should not expect a library page to have the answer to an involved research question.

Within the library are clerks, staff assistants, secretaries, pages, student workers, and librarians. The librarian is a professional with a minimum of an accredited master's degree in library science. Most institutions of higher education have the same requirements for a librarian as for a member of the teaching faculty, and a second master's degree is often required for tenure.

Libraries are organized in many different ways, depending on their size and the needs of the patrons or institution they serve. But generally speaking, libraries are organized into two broad areas: technical services and public services.

Technical Services

Technical services staff can be thought of as those who work behind the scenes. They are the ones responsible for ordering the materials (though not necessarily deciding which materials to order) and handling them from the time they arrive at the delivery dock until they are on the shelf. Technical services is divided into several major areas:

Acquisitions. Those in the acquisitions department actually place the orders for the materials with the various publishers and suppliers. When the materials arrive, it is their responsibility to receive them, make sure that the order has arrived as requested, and pass along the invoices for payment and the materials for processing.

Cataloging. The cataloging department is responsible for the organization of the collection. Its duty is to see that materials on the same subject are grouped together on the shelf to make it easier for the patron to find them. Therefore, the staff classifies the materials and assigns call numbers according to whichever classification system the library uses. (In the United States, that is usually the Dewey Decimal System or the Library of Congress System.)

The cataloging department is responsible for preparing entries for each item for the card catalog or the automated catalog and filing the cards in the drawers or adding the information to the database. It is also responsible for the process in reverse—removing entries from the catalog for materials that have been lost or discarded.

Processing. Some libraries have a processing department that is responsible for the physical preparation of the material. They do such tasks as applying spine labels and barcodes, inserting book pockets, and placing plastic jackets on the books.

Mending and binding. This department, sometimes combined with and sometimes separate from processing, is responsible for the physical well-being of the materials. Worn and torn materials are mended and repaired. While larger libraries may have their own in-house bindery, most libraries send materials needing extensive repair to an outside bindery. It is the responsibility of this department to get them there and back.

Serials. Serials are materials that come at repeated intervals—such as yearbooks or magazines. This department is responsible for receiving the materials when they arrive, checking them in, and getting them to the shelf. It is also this department's responsibility to notice materials that fail to arrive and contact the supplier. In large libraries, periodicals (magazines and journals) may be a separate department from or a subdivision of the serials department.

Public Services

The people in public services are the ones you will usually see in your visits to the library. Their primary function is to assist you, the patron.

Circulation. One of the major subdivisions of the public services department is the circulation department. This department is primarily responsible for checking out materials to the borrower and getting them back. When materials are returned, it is their job to get them back to the proper shelf. If the library uses a fine system, they must collect the fines for overdue materials. If materials are not returned, it is the responsibility of the circulation department to contact the recalcitrant borrower and, occasionally, turn over the case to a collection agency.

Reserve. The reserve book department may be contained within or be separate from the circulation department. A professor may make a reading assignment for an entire class (or several classes) in the same book. If there is only one copy of the book in the library and someone checks it out, no one else gets a chance to read the assignment. To avoid this, the professor may choose to place the book on reserve. Reserve simply means that the book is placed on limited circulation. Instead of being checked out for the usual two, three or four weeks at a time (whatever the policy of the library is), the book may now be checked out only for overnight use or for two hours use within the library. (Again, this time period varies according to the policy of each library and the wishes of the professor.) Its purpose is to make a limited number of materials available to the greatest number of users in the shortest period of time.

Reference. The reference department is probably the department (other than circulation) that the researcher will deal with the most. Though some people find it difficult to believe, libraries actually pay someone for sitting at a desk and answering questions. This person is available and waiting to be asked.

The reference librarian is one of the most highly trained individuals in the library. It is he or she who knows the collection and the tools for accessing it. The reference librarian with a second master's may also be a scholar in his or her own particular academic discipline and can be the researcher's single most valuable asset.

While it is impossible for an individual reference librarian to be an expert in every single subject area in which someone may require assistance, he or she is trained in the techniques of locating and evaluating information. Though the sources are not the same for all disciplines, the techniques are. The reference librarian is trained in the basic sources for all disciplines or at least knows which tools to use to find them. Larger libraries have a staff of reference librarians, each with his or her own subject specialties; if one cannot help, possibly another can.

Before approaching the reference librarian, there is a basic supposition that must be understood: This individual is there to help you do your work, not to do it for you. Exhaust your own resources before asking for assistance so that you may say, "I've looked in the catalog for books on the Protestant Reformation, but I couldn't find any. Am I looking under the right subject heading?" rather than "What have you got on the Reformation?"

Expect the reference librarian to answer your question with a question. He is trained to elicit as much information from you as possible so that he may be as specific as possible in finding the answer you want. He is not trying to pry, only to be specific. If the information you are researching is confidential, say so. Reference librarians do not care what you are researching, but they do need as much information as you can give them so they can be sure of finding the right answer for you.

After the librarian has helped you, if the answer is not what you need, feel free to say, "Thank you, but that's not quite what I'm looking for. Is there another source that we could check?" The reference librarian wants to find the answer, but often doesn't know if he's succeeded unless you tell him.

Be courteous in your use of the reference librarian's time. The reference desk, particularly in an academic library, can be extremely busy. It is not unusual in some libraries to see four or five people in line and two phones ringing at the same time. Try to keep your query as brief and simple as possible. If your question requires an in-depth answer that is going to take some time, schedule your time at the reference desk when it is less busy. Some reference desks will even make an appointment for you to have a lengthy session with the person who is most skilled in your subject area.

Undergraduate students are known for not beginning their work on time. Reference librarians often hear: "I have this term paper due tomorrow and I need five sources." Locating information takes time. After it is found, it most likely will not be in the form needed for the final paper or project. It is going to take some time for the researcher to pull it together and reorganize it. The responsibility of the reference librarian ends with locating the information; pulling it all together in final form is the responsibility of the student or researcher.

It is fair to expect the reference librarian to teach you how to use the catalog or to show you where the materials are found. It is not fair to ask the librarian to look up every book or to retrieve it for you. If you do not understand something about the library, ask, but ask with the goal of learning to do it for yourself.

Telephone reference. Many libraries offer telephone reference service. These libraries will take a phone call and give you a specific piece of information over the phone. By all means, use the service, but do not abuse it.

Keep your phone query to a simple fact or two. The telephone reference staff will be glad to tell you the current population of Paris or whether or not the library has a certain book (and in some cases whether it is checked out or not), but do not expect them to have time to read you a four-page essay over the phone.

If it sounds as though the library is busy, keep your phone query brief or ask if there is a more convenient time for you to call back. Traffic at the reference desk goes in spurts: The librarian may sit for ten or fifteen minutes with no questions and suddenly six people approach at the same time—all of them with lengthy requests. Most libraries give priority to the patron who has put forth the effort to go in person over the one making a convenient phone call from home. For questions that are a little lengthy, some libraries will be glad to take your phone number and call you back.

Interlibrary loan. If the library doesn't own the book you need or seems to have nothing on your topic, ask the reference librarian if they have interlibrary loan service. This service provides access to books from other libraries where you would not normally be allowed borrowing privileges. Again, be as specific as possible with your request. Some libraries will only handle a request for a specific book, while others are prepared to fill a more general request for "any information" on a given topic.

Always allow two to three weeks for an interlibrary loan request. Remember that your library is at the mercy of the lending library, so do not get upset with your library if the book is slow in coming. Ask what the usual response time is; then, if you haven't heard by that time, inquire again.

If the length of time you may keep the material is short, that has been determined by the lending library, not by your library. If renewals are not allowed, that is the policy of the lender, not of your library.

Online reference. Another department under the umbrella of Public Services may be the online reference department. It may be called "online searching," "information retrieval," or a myriad of other names. Many of the indexes that were previously available only in paper form, plus many new ones, are now available in electronic format. Depending on the complexity of your search and the type of information you need, this may be the quickest and best way to locate the information. If you think you might need the service, ask if it is available. For more information on online searching, see the section "Online Search Services" in Chapter Five.

Bibliographic instruction. Larger libraries often have a department devoted specifically to bibliographic instruction—teaching about books and libraries, your library in particular. It is this department that conducts the orientation tours for the new students and provides materials to professors for use in teaching about the library in the classroom. If you want to learn how to use the library to your best advantage, someone from this department can work with you.

Periodicals. Another major department is periodicals. We discussed previously the portion of the periodicals department that is responsible for receiving the materials and getting them to the shelves. This is the portion that handles the materials once they are on the shelf and available to the user.

Periodicals are generally divided into two sections: current and bound. An explanation follows:

> **Current periodicals**. In many libraries, the current issues are in an area by themselves. Many libraries simply place the materials on the shelf in alphabetical order by the title of the magazine or journal. Some libraries, however, classify them and assign a call number so that all journals on the same subject are shelved near each other. In this case, you will need to use a catalog to find the call number so you can locate the journal.
>
> The type of catalog used for journals varies from library to library. Some libraries simply keep a printed list or a computer printout listing the journals that are held. Often, additional information is given, such as the volume numbers and dates of each title owned by the library. Other libraries use a "visible file," which is a kind of chart listing the titles in alphabetical sequence. Each title is held in a strip of plastic and the chart may be updated with relative ease as titles are added or dropped. Still other libraries list their journals in the main library catalog, so that the user may go there to find out if the library owns a particular title.
>
> **Bound periodicals**. Older materials are often moved to a separate area of the library.[1] Some libraries bind their magazines so that the issues stay together in order and are easier to shelve and locate. To many new users the shelves look like they are full of books, but a glance inside the covers will show that they are just the magazines we are familiar with, sewn together at the spine, and with a hard cover added to them.
>
> Other libraries simply box the materials so that the issues of a given volume are shelved together in the same box. And some libraries discard their paper copies of journals altogether and keep back issues only on microfilm or microfiche. Within a given library, it is not unusual to find materials treated all four ways: some bound, some boxed, some on microfilm, and some on microfiche.

Depending on the library, the section for bound journals may be a special section housing only journals, as is often the case. Some libraries, however, classify and catalog the older issues just as they would a book. So, a religion journal will be found shelved in the regular stacks right next to the religion books.

Periodicals indexes. Somewhere near the periodicals you will usually find the periodicals indexes. If you are trying to find an article on Paul Tillich, for example, you could just go to a journal where you think the article might have appeared and flip through issues until you found it, but such a procedure would probably require a great deal of time and effort unless you were sure of the exact journal and knew the issue it appeared in. A much easier way is to locate a periodicals index and look under "Tillich, Paul" or whatever subject you need to locate. There you will find the title of the journal the article appeared in, its author, the issue it appeared in, and the numbers of the pages on which it appeared. We will discuss periodicals indexes in greater depth in Chapter Four.

Government documents. Many libraries, especially larger ones, have a collection of government documents. Despite the awe-inspiring title, these are nothing more than a collection of items that are published by federal, state, and local government bodies. Each year government organizations publish many thousands of documents. Some libraries are defined as "depository libraries," which means they automatically receive all or a selected portion of these items. Because there are so many items, it could be a time-consuming and overwhelming task to classify all of them and add them to the regular collection. So some libraries simply designate a special area for them and use the classification scheme that has been established by the government. While quite different from the Dewey or Library of Congress systems, it is no more difficult, and the researcher should learn to use it early if he or she will need government publications in the research process—and chances are most of us will.

In addition to the previously mentioned departments, which are in almost every library, your library may have other special departments. Sometimes these are classed under the title of "Special Collections" and may include rare books; the university archives; denominational archives, if the institution is affiliated with a particular religious body; the collected works of a particular author; a genealogy collection; or a local history collection. There are many types of special collections and some may be unique to an institution. Ask which ones your library has.

Endnote

1. The definition of "older" varies widely from one library to another, but, very generally, it means anything prior to the current year.

Chapter Two

The Library Catalog

Just as the telescope allows us to pick out and focus on a particular star in the heavens, so the library catalog is an instrument that allows us to pick out and focus on the information we need from within the vast resources of the library.

The library catalog provides multiple points of access to the library collection: The primary points are author, title, and subject. Some libraries have an online catalog that also allows searching by keyword. Let us look first at the traditional card catalog.

The Card Catalog

Some libraries use a dictionary-style card catalog in which all three types of cards—author, title and subject—are filed in a single alphabet. Other libraries use a divided catalog with each type of card filed in a separate alphabet in a separate cabinet or set of cabinets. In other libraries, author and title cards are filed together and subject cards are filed in a separate alphabet. It is vital for the researcher to know which type of system a library uses before beginning research.

It is also important to know which style of filing system the library uses. Most libraries use word-by-word filing and follow a rule called the "nothing before something" rule. In a word-by-word system, for example, the subject "New York" would file before "Newark" or "Newsweek" because nothing—the blank space between the two words—files before something—the letter "a" or the letter "s." This rule is becoming increasingly important to understand with the advent of automation because a computer will alphabetize "nothing" before "something."

Another important filing rule is the "by before about" rule. All the books *by* an author are filed in the catalog *before* books *about* him. Likewise, a book written by "Brown, Zelda" would file before a book entitled *The Brown Boat*.

There is also a hierarchy of filing rules as to which comes first of commas, periods, colons, semicolons, and hyphens. Generally, a library user need not be concerned with such intricate detail other than to know that if you do not find the book listed where you think it should be, try another likely spot. If you still have trouble locating a book, inquire which system your library uses or ask the reference librarian for help.

The Catalog Card

The individual unit of the catalog is the catalog card. Being able to read and understand the information contained on a card will unleash great research power.

A card is divided into paragraphs. Each paragraph is indented and contains specific information. Author, title, and subject cards are virtually alike, but different information is printed at the top of the card.

Author. Figure 2.1 is a sample of a catalog card for Cruden's *Concordance*. The first paragraph of a catalog card always begins with the (1) last name of the author, if there is an author. This card is what we call an author card. Note that the (2) birth and death dates of the author are sometimes given. This helps the researcher distinguish between people of the same name. (Try looking in the catalog of a large library for John Kennedy.) The author card is usually called the "main entry" and may sometimes contain more information than a similar title or subject card. When there is no author, the title of the work appears first and the title card is considered the main entry.

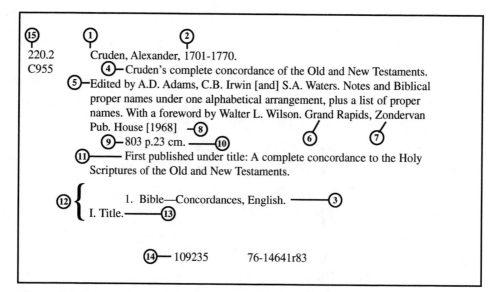

Figure 2.1   Sample of a catalog card for Cruden's *Concordance*

Subject. If this were a subject card, the (3) subject "Bible-Concordances, English" would be written at the very top of the card above the author paragraph in all capital letters. Some catalogs still contain older cards on which the subjects were typed at the top using red ink, but current practice is to use all caps. Either red ink or all-caps indicates that this is the subject, not the title, of the book. A subject may be a topic per se, or it may be the name of a person, place, or thing.

Title. Below the author's name, and indented, is the (4) title of the book. If this were a title card, the title would be repeated at the top of the card above the author's name. Note that the title is neither typed in red nor in all capital letters and that only the first word and proper nouns are capitalized. (This style of noncapitalization is followed simply to increase the cataloger's typing speed by not having to press the "shift" key repeatedly.)

Statement of responsibility. Immediately following the title and in the same paragraph is what is called the statement of responsibility, which is usually a repetition of the author's name and may include co-authors, (5) editors or illustrators. Next, and in the same paragraph, is the imprint. The imprint is information specific to this edition of the book. If this is at least the second edition of a book, it will list here which edition this is. The imprint contains the (6) publisher's location, the (7) publisher's name, and the (8) copyright date of the book. The researcher can use information from the imprint to determine the nationality of a publication. A book published in Ireland may not give a proper perspective of some American event, but it may be the best source for something that occurred in Ireland. A glance at the publisher's name may tell the researcher something about the quality of this book. And the copyright date will show how current the information is.

Collation. The paragraph after the imprint is the collation. If the paragraph begins with a lower-case Roman numeral, that tells how many pages of introductory material are contained in the work. (9) An Arabic numeral shows the number of pages in the body of the work. The statement "il.," "ill.," or "illus." indicates that the look contains illustrations. If you must have a picture of the person or subject you are researching and this statement is absent, obviously you should look for another source. Often the statement is so specific as to indicate that the book contains maps, charts, graphs or other specific types of illustrative material. And finally, many cards give the (10) height of the book in centimeters. Generally of interest to librarians for shelving purposes, this statement may give you an overall idea of the size of the book you are dealing with. You won't want to plan on walking home or riding the bus with a stack of books that is 96 centimeters tall.

Notes. Following the collation is the (11) notes paragraph. If the book has an index or a bibliography, it is listed here. Many cards list the page number on that this information is given. With this information, a researcher can quickly locate a book that he might have bypassed as of no value for his project, but he may discover that the bibliography may prove invaluable in locating further sources (or "primary" or original sources) on the subject. Some cards may give additional notes about the work such as a brief summary of the book or some type of information particular to this edition, or even this copy, such as "autographed by the author." This note on Cruden's *Concordance* shows that the concordance was originally published under another title.

Tracings. The last paragraph on the card is called the (12) tracing. Those items that appear following Arabic numerals are subject headings under which this book is listed in the card catalog. They are extremely helpful to the researcher wishing to locate similar books or other books on the same topic. Simply make note of what seems to be a promising subject heading and look in the catalog under that heading. Items that appear after Roman numerals are called (13) "added entries" and refer to such things as co-authors, illustrators, alternate titles or the series of which the book forms a part, if any. The researcher wishing to find similar books might want to look elsewhere in the catalog under the name of the co-author or the series.

The information at the (14) bottom of the card does not always appear. Its appearance depends upon who produced the card, is generally of interest to library staff only, and may be ignored by the researcher.

Call number. Finally, in the upper left-hand corner of the card is the (15) "call number," which tells where the book is located on the shelf. In most libraries in the United States, this number will belong either to the Dewey Decimal system or the Library of Congress system.

A Dewey number will have a first line that consists of numerals only with exactly three digits to the left of the decimal point. The second line is a Cutter number, which is a mixture of letters and numbers representing the author's last name and the title of the work. Generally speaking, a Cutter number will begin with a capital letter (the first letter of the author's last name) followed by two or three digits, followed by a lower-case letter, which is the first letter of the first significant word of the title.

Some libraries simply use the first three letters of the author's last name instead of a true Cutter number.

A typical Dewey call number would appear like this:

Subject number   618.2

Cutter number   M484r

An LC (*Library of Congress*) number will consist of a subject number, comprised of both letters and numerals and a Cutter number. An LC number always begins with a letter or two. The Cutter number is preceded by a decimal point. (An LC number may contain several decimal points, while a Dewey number may contain only one.) A typical LC number would appear thus:

Subject number   PS613

Cutter number   .W47

In both systems the Cutter number is treated as a decimal, so that on the shelf a book with the LC number "PS613.W47" would come before "PS613.W5." A book with the Dewey number "618.2 M484r" would come before "618.2 M53j."

For a basic introduction to the library and classification systems, the researcher is well advised to take a careful look at Jean Key Gates' *Guide to the Use of Libraries and Information Sources*, 7th edition (New York: McGraw-Hill, 1994) and the *Dewey Decimal Classification and Relative Index,* edition 21 (New York: Forest Press, 1996).

The Library of Congress Classification System

In 1897 the task of recataloging and reclassifying the Library of Congress was begun. The Library of Congress Classification System, which was developed in that process, combines letters of the alphabet and Arabic numerals; it provides for the most minute groupings of subjects through the combination of letters and numerals; it is designed for libraries with very large collections. The letters I, O, W, X, and Y are not used but are left for further expansion or are used in complementary classification systems such as the *National Library of Medicine*.

A brief outline of the Library of Congress Classification System follows:

A   General Works

B   Philosophy, Psychology, Religion

C   Auxiliary Sciences of History

D   History: General and Old World

E-F   History: America

G   Geography, Anthropology, Recreation

H   Social Sciences

J   Political Science

K   Law

L   Education

M   Music and Books on Music

N   Fine Arts

P   Language and Literature

Q   Science

R   Medicine

S   Agriculture

T   Technology

U   Military Science

V   Naval Science

Z   Library Science

The major subdivisions for religion and philosophy are:

BC   Logic

BD   Speculative Philosophy

BJ   Ethics

BL   Religions, Mythology, Rationalism

BM   Judaism

BP   Islam, Bahaism, Theosophy, etc.

BQ   Buddhism

BR   Christianity

BS   The Bible

BT   Doctrinal Theology

BV   Practical Theology

BX   Christian Denominations

While are many other subcategories within these divisions, these will give the researcher some exposure to the sophistication and detailed specialization that library science has brought to the cataloging of books in modern times.

The Dewey Decimal Classification System

In the Dewey Decimal Classification System, Arabic numerals are used to signify the various classes of subjects. It was created by an early American librarian, Melvil Dewey, who divided all knowledge, as represented by books and other materials, into nine classes, which he numbered 100 to 900. Materials too general to belong in a specific group, such as encyclopedias, dictionaries, newspapers, handbooks, and the like, he placed in a tenth class, which precedes the others as the 000 class. Every researcher should know these ten categories. They are part of the basic knowledge of research, and the researcher will use this information at every library using the Dewey Decimal Classification System. These ten major categories are:

000	General Works
100	Philosophy
200	Religion
⁓ 300	Social Sciences
400	Language
500	Pure Science
600	Technology, Applied Science
700	The Arts
800	Literature
900	History, Biography

The system progresses from the preceding ten general classifications to more and more precise subclassifications, based on a decade arrangement. Each of the previously mentioned ten categories is again divided into ten subcategories, thus providing 100 slots into which books may be classified. Each of these 100 slots is again divided into ten further classification areas.

Usually, this three-digit thousand category is followed by a decimal point, after which the subdividing continues. As noted previously, the major category for religion is the 200s. Religion is generally broken down into these ten major subcategories:

210	Natural religion
220	Bible
230	Christian doctrinal theology
240	Christian moral and devotional works
250	Local church and religious orders
260	Social and ecclesiastical theology
270	History and geography of the church

280   Christian denominations and sects

290   Other religions and comparative religion

Both systems are simply ways of classifying information so that books on a given topic are placed near each other on the shelf. This, in turn, makes it easier for the user to locate other books on the chosen subject. While smaller libraries tend to use Dewey and larger libraries LC, there is no rule, and it actually makes little difference to the user.

Some libraries handle biography and autobiography a little differently from other types of nonfiction. Instead of being assigned a call number, biographies may simply be marked with a "B" and shelved in a separate section. Other libraries use "921" or simply a "92" (from the Dewey Decimal system) to indicate biography. Usually they are filed by last name of the subject (not the author) so that all biographies about Lincoln would appear together on the shelf. If biographies are not where it seems they should be, ask where they are shelved.

Some libraries shelve fiction in a separate section. Instead of a call number, an "F" or "Fic" is given for the call number, and the books are then filed by author's last name in the fiction section. Other libraries do not bother to indicate "F" or "Fic", and the call number appears blank, indicating simply that books are filed in the fiction section by author's last name. In some libraries, some works of fiction may be classified as literature and shelved with the regular collection under the appropriate call number for literature.

Where do you begin if you do not know what the proper subject heading is for a topic? How do you know whether to look under "Railroad trains," "Trains," "Trains, Railroad," "Passenger trains," "Passenger service–rail," "Trains, Passenger," or "Railroads, Passenger"? If library catalogers were to file a card under whatever subject heading appealed to them at the moment, it would be difficult to locate all the books in the library on a given subject, particularly as there are staff changes in the cataloging department over the years. Therefore, catalogers use a guide entitled *Library of Congress Subject Headings* for the express purpose of providing standardization. If you're not sure what the proper subject heading is, look in *LCSH*— a large red book, usually in two volumes—under what you feel is the most likely subject heading. *LCSH* provides ample cross-references to the correct heading. (Proper headings are printed in **Boldface** print.) Many libraries keep a copy of *LCSH* near the library catalog or at the reference desk. If you do not see a copy of *LCSH*, ask at the reference desk.

The online catalog. Many libraries have now automated their catalogs. Automation allows greater flexibility in manipulating information and a larger number of access points for the user. Some systems even contain circulation information so the user knows immediately if the desired book is on the shelf or checked out. Often the information on the computer screen will look similar to that on a catalog card. All the information available on a catalog card is available on the screen of an online system (see Figure 2.2). The display format for online data has not yet been standardized so the researcher must learn to locate the desired information on whatever system is in use.

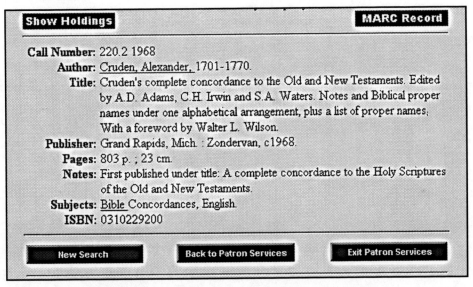

Figure 2.2   Sample of an online card catalog screen

The online catalog has several advantages over the card catalog. First of all, the online catalog is easier to maintain. While that might seem to be of no consequence to the researcher, it is an important advantage. Because keeping a card catalog up-to-date (inserting new cards and removing those for lost or discarded items) is very labor-intensive, the card catalog is seldom truly up-to-date. The online catalog, however, may be up-to-the-minute because the cataloging librarian can create the electronic record for an item and instantly add it to the database (see Figure 2.3 on page 18 for another sample presentation). Likewise, missing or discarded items can be promptly removed from the database.

The online catalog harnesses the power of the computer for the researcher's advantage. In the traditional card catalog, the researcher had only three entry points: the name of the

```
┌──────────────────────────────────────────────────────────────────────┐
│  LONG VIEW                                                             │
│ ···················································································· │
│             | Help | New Title Search | Return to Title List | Search Menu |        │
│ ···················································································· │
│        Author  Cruden, Alexander, 1701-1770.                          │
│          Title  Complete concordance to the Old and New Testaments. Edited by A.D. Adams, C.H. Irwin and S.A. Waters. │
│      Published  Grand Rapids, Zondervan Pub. House 1955, c1949         │
│    Description  vii, 800 p. 22 cm.                                     │
│       Subjects  Bible--Concordances, English.                         │
│ ···················································································· │
│       Location  IUPUI UNIV LIB                                        │
│    Call Number  BS425 .C8 1955                                        │
│         Status  In Library. If unable to locate, ask for assistance.  │
│ ···················································································· │
│             | Help | New Title Search | Return to Title List | Search Menu |        │
└──────────────────────────────────────────────────────────────────────┘
```

Figure 2.3   Another sample of an online card catalog screen

author, the title of the work, or the subject of the work. A researcher trying to locate a specific work in a card catalog must know either its author or its title. Furthermore, he or she must know the first word of the title. In order to locate the *Twentieth Century Encyclopedia of Religious Knowledge* in the card catalog, the researcher would have to know that the first word of the title is "Twentieth." Looking under "Century," "Encyclopedia," or "Religious" would yield nothing. In the online catalog, however, the researcher could enter any of those words or some combination thereof and likely locate the work quickly and easily.

An online catalog allows many other entry points, for example, keywords from a particular part of the record (called a *field*) or from all fields. As in the title search mentioned previously, if the researcher has some idea what the work is about, he or she can search for keywords from the subject field. For example, to locate the *Twentieth Century Encyclopedia of Religious Knowledge* in the online catalog, the researcher could search for the keywords "dictionary" and "theology" in the subject field without having to know that the exact "approved" subject heading is "Theology—Dictionaries."

The online catalog allows the researcher to limit the search. For example, if the researcher knows that the word "dictionary" appears in the title of the work, he could limit the search for the word specifically to the title field, thereby excluding all those works that had the word "dictionary" only in the subject field.

The online catalog allows the user to search many fields that could not be indexed in the traditional card catalog, for example the "notes" field. This field often contains a short summary or abstract of the work and may contain important clues to locating it.

By searching the notes, the researcher may be able to locate a book that he would not have been able to find in a card catalog.

Fields can be combined in specific ways in an online search. For example, the search can specify that the work must contain the name "Melton" in the author field and the word "American" in the title field.

Searches may also be limited in order to find works germane to the topic more easily. A search can be limited by date (e.g. works prior to 1956) or by language (e.g., works in German only). Some catalogs allow searching or limiting by other fields such as publisher, place of publication, or even the number of pages. In brief, the online catalog allows the user to tailor a search to locate only those resources most relevant to the research topic.

Another item of information given in the online catalog is shelf status of the sought-after work. The researcher can tell while still at the catalog if the work is on the shelf, checked out (and sometimes, when it is due back), missing, or on order. The user of the card catalog, meanwhile, must note the location of each item and go to the library shelves to see if it is available. If the item is not on the shelf, he must then ask the library staff if the item is checked out, missing, etc. The online catalog will save the researcher much time and frustration.

If the needed item is not on the shelf, the researcher using an online catalog can often place a hold on the item. Thus, when it is returned to the library, the library staff will notify the researcher that the item is now available. Some automation systems will allow the user to place the hold directly; in other systems, the user must request the library staff to do it on his behalf.

Whichever system your library uses, introduce yourself early and become familiar with it. A couple of hours "playing" in the library will be an invaluable timesaver when there is a research deadline to be met.

Chapter Three

The Reference Collection— Tomes of Information

Due to a lack of basic research skills, a beginning researcher may assume the library deficient in materials when, in reality, there is a mountain of literature that is inaccessible to the untrained user. Nowhere in the library is there to be found such a concentration of research materials as in the reference department. Here, among other resources, are to be found many kinds of dictionaries, encyclopedias, government documents, and a full range of indices. We will discuss these groupings later, but first, let us take a closer look at reference books in general.

Evaluating a Reference Book

What is a reference book? What distinguishes it from a nonreference book?

A primary distinction is revealed by the term itself. A reference book is not intended to be read from cover to cover like a novel or a biography, but is referred to in order to locate specific factual information. The information is usually, but not always, brief in nature.

Having determined what a reference book is, how does one determine what a good reference book is? There are a number of criteria that may be applied.

First of all, read the introductory material. Usually there is a section (or sections) at the beginning of the work, which tells its purpose, its scope, and briefly outlines it contents. Knowing the authors' purpose, we can then apply other criteria to decide whether or not they fulfill that purpose.

Scope. The scope of a book is its span of coverage. In order to locate information efficiently, we must determine whether a particular book deals adequately with the topic we are investigating. A book entitled *America in the Twenties* would probably be limited to a discussion of things happening in America during the 1920s and would not be our primary text for research on European current events during World War II. Its scope includes neither the topic we are researching (Europe) nor the time period (World War II.)

Bias. Merriam-Webster defines bias as "an inclination of temperament or outlook; especially: a personal and *sometimes* unreasoned judgment."[1] Bias is not always a negative term. Bias is simply the author's feelings toward his subject. However, when an author's point of view is limited by the purposeful exclusion of any evidence that disagrees with his opinion, we can say that he is biased.

The distinction between a biased work and an unbiased one is sometimes thin, but essentially if an author presents his viewpoint as one of several viewpoints to be considered, we can say the work is unbiased. If he presents his viewpoint as the only and absolute truth, willfully excluding or ignoring abundant evidence to the contrary, we can say the work is biased. In researching the history of a particular denomination, for example, a text written by a member of that denomination may be the best source, for a member can have a feeling and an appreciation for the denomination that an outsider cannot. If, however, the author's zeal for promoting the denomination distorts the facts, a text written by an outside party may be the best source.

Point of view. Every book has a point of view. In order to determine whether a book suits our research purpose, we must determine what is its point of view. The author might be looking at his subject from either the inside or the outside—a member of a denomination or an outsider writing its history. His purpose might be to convert or simply to lay down the facts. An author's timeframe is also a point of view. A book like *America in the Twenties* could either be a look at current events or a historical perspective of the decade, depending upon when it was written and the point of view of the author. Either point of view is valid, but one or the other may not suit our purpose. In choosing a reference book, we must make sure that the author's point of view is appropriate to the subject and to our needs.

Copyright. The copyright date of a work can often tell us immediately if it is the source we need. If the piece of information we need is the current membership of Pentecostal churches in Latin America, a book with a 1967 copyright date will give us the wrong information. Though perfectly correct when the book was published, time has made the information false if we need a current figure. On the other hand, if we are charting growth over the years, the 1967 figure may be exactly the one we need.

Index. Is the work indexed? Check the back of the book (or rarely, the front) to see if there is an index. Many otherwise potentially useful books are worth less than the paper they are written on because the information they contain is virtually inaccessible.

Organization. Is the book organized chronologically? Geographically? Alphabetically? By topic? Poor organization can waste much of a researcher's time. If we need information on the growth of the church in Latin America, a chronological (but not geographical) organization could waste hours as we have to search through data on all the other countries of the world seeking those items that refer only to Latin America. Likewise, a strictly geographical organization might not show us the progress of growth over time. If we want to chart growth country by country, a work that gives statistics only by region will not give us the information we need. In any of these cases it might be better to find another work whose organization more exactly fits our needs.

Author's credentials. Finally, take a look at the credentials of the author. Has he or she written on this topic before? What has his experience in the field been? Has he based his work on that of others who have been prominent in the field? If so, has he agreed or disagreed with them? Has he added to their discoveries, or merely rehashed them? How have others in the field regarded his work? What do the critics say? If you know that the author is someone whose viewpoint is vastly different from yours, you probably will not find much support in his works for the argument you are trying to present.

While it may require a little extra effort, taking some additional time to find the appropriate source can often be a timesaver over taking the first source that comes along.

Let us now look at some specific types of reference materials.

Dictionaries

The major "unabridged" English-language dictionaries most useful to the researcher are *Webster's New International Dictionary of the English Language*, *Webster's Third New International Dictionary*, or *Funk and Wagnall's New Standard Dictionary*. For studying word origins, the standard is the *Oxford English Dictionary* (OED).

It should be noted here that "Webster's" is a generic term coming from Noah Webster, compiler of an early dictionary, and can be used by anyone. Merriam-Webster is a reputable dictionary publisher, producer of the *Third New International Dictionary* mentioned previously. If you find it confusing to distinguish one "Webster's" from another, that is just what some not-so-reputable publishers want. Just because it is a "Webster's" dictionary is no sign that it is a good one.

Major components of language dictionaries include spelling, etymologies (the history of a word), definitions, pronunciation, synonyms, syllabication, and grammatical information.

Specialized Dictionaries in Religious Studies

In addition to language dictionaries, there is a wide range of specialized subject dictionaries that the informed researcher will want to become acquainted with, and these may be found in the reference section.

Dictionary of Pentecostal and Charismatic Movements. Stanley M. Burgess and Gary B, McGee, eds. Grand Rapids, MI: Zondervan, 1993, 1988. 950 pp.

The Interpreter's Dictionary of the Bible. George Arthur Buttrick, ed. Nashville, TN: Abingdon Press, 1976. 4 volumes.

The Oxford Dictionary of the Christian Church, 3rd ed. F. L. Cross, ed. New York: Oxford University Press, 1998, 1997.

Theological Dictionary of the Old Testament. Revised edition. G. Johannes Botterweck & Helmet Ringgren, eds. Grand Rapids, MI: Eerdmans, 1997. 7 volumes.

Theological Dictionary of the New Testament. Gerhard Kittel and Gerhard Friedrich, eds. Grand Rapids, MI: William B. Eerdmans, 1983, 1984. 9 volumes.

Encyclopedias

There is more than one kind of encyclopedia, even though many undergraduate students have been nurtured with the notion that either the ***Encyclopedia Americana*** or ***The World Book*** (or, if the student is particularly interested in specialized knowledge, the ***Encyclopaedia Britannica***) constitute the full range. Though these are very valuable sources of general information, the religion student serious about library research will seek out specialized encyclopedias that will prove to be the most valuable of all. Nevertheless, general encyclopedias do have a great deal of merit.

General Encyclopedias

"For your research paper, you must use three different sources and you cannot use an encyclopedia." Surely every student has heard this from his teacher many times over during elementary and high school. Why the bias against encyclopedias? Are they inherently evil? What's wrong with them?

Actually, nothing is basically wrong with using encyclopedias—the good ones anyway—if they are used properly. But fifth graders (and sometimes university students and seminarians) tend to rely on them too completely. Encyclopedias are often like distilled water—the essence is there, but not the flavor. Students use them heavily because they want their research pre-digested for them rather than doing it themselves from primary sources. So, why do encyclopedias exist? Who should use them and when? How should they be used?

Encyclopedias are a ready-reference source—a handy place for quick information. They provide a broad overview of popular subjects of general interest (hence the term "general interest encyclopedia"). The articles in an encyclopedia are written by experts in the field and are aimed at those who are not.

Encyclopedias can serve the specialist by providing a summary of his or her discipline, or the novice by providing an introduction. They are a good starting point. The novice doing research on Louis XIV can get an idea of when and where he lived and who he was from the general encyclopedia. That information, at least, will tell us that we probably will not find much about him in a book on avant-garde theater in Buenos Aires, but surely will find him in books on the history of France.

If we learn from the encyclopedia that John Doe is an author and is currently living, we know to look next in reference works on contemporary authors. From the encyclopedia we learn that the Haversian canals are an anatomical, not a geographical, feature and that Menno Simons is a name we'll want to be on the lookout for while studying the history of the Mennonites.

The encyclopedia can also be useful as a bibliographic tool. Some encyclopedias list books and articles for further reading on the topic. Check the introductory material for the encyclopedia to see if bibliographies are given and if they are with the articles or in a separate section. Rather than wonder if the library has "any books on XYZ," the prepared researcher will have a list of books and can go directly to the catalog to see if the library has them.

When using the encyclopedia, always approach the topic through the index, rather than by the grammar school method of grabbing the appropriate volume and looking directly for the article. Louis XIV may be listed in the "L" volume; or he may not be. But the researcher who looks only in the "L" volume rather than in the index will surely miss many other references to him in articles on the history of France and other topics.

Use the encyclopedia. Use it often. But use it well. And use it only as a starting point for further research.

Specialized Encyclopedias in Religious Studies

The Encyclopedia of Philosophy. Paul Edwards, ed. New York: Simon & Schuster Macmillan, 1996. 8 volumes.

Encyclopedia of Religion and Ethics. James Hastings, editor. New York: Charles Scribner, 1980. 13 volumes.

Encyclopedia of Theology: The Concise Sacramentum Mundi. Karl Rahner, ed. Tunbridge Wells: Burns & Oates, 1993, 1975.

The Jewish Encyclopedia. New York: Funk and Wagnalls, 1983. 12 volumes.

The New Schaff-Herzog Encyclopedia of Religious Knowledge. Samuel Macauley Jackson, editor-in-chief. Grand Rapids, MI: Baker Book House, 1977. 15 volumes.

Beyond these specialized encyclopedias, several major concordances, commentaries and handbooks are also listed in the Appendix.

Government Documents

Though the government documents section of the reference collection is problematical and complex, the researcher in religion and theology may occasionally refer to these documents. Initially, you might wish to consult one of these two sources for a general overview of the available materials, namely Joe Morehead's *Introduction to United States Public Documents,* 3rd edition, (Littleton, CO: Libraries Unlimited, Inc., 1983, 309 pp.) or Laurence F. Schmeckebier and Roy Be Eastin's *Government Publications and Their Use* (2nd revised edition, Washington, DC: The Brookings Institute, 1986, 502 pp.).

An important tool used in locating United States government documents is the *Monthly Catalog of U.S. Government Publications* (United States Superintendent of Documents, 1895 to date) because it is the single most comprehensive listing of all unclassified publications issued by the various departments and agencies of the United States government. Another reference of major importance because it offers a comprehensive annotated guide to the series and periodicals produced by agencies and departments of the United States government is Donna Batten's *Guide to U.S. Government Publications* (Farmington Hills, MI: The Gale Group, 2000). For further listings, library staff will be happy to show you many of these sources and their primary method of use.

Indexes

An indispensable category of reference works for the researcher of religion and theology is the index. As these sources generally index primarily periodicals and journals—although they sometimes include books and other types of material—and are often shelved with or near the periodicals, they are discussed in Chapter Four.

Endnote

1. *WWWebster Dictionary, WWWDictionary.* Merriam-Webster. **http://www.m-w.com/cgi-bin/ dictionary** April 1, 2000.

Periodicals and Indexes

Periodicals

Some students are of the false impression that the library subscribes to magazines and newspapers just to keep the library user happy. That is, the magazines and various other loose items lying near and shelved close to comfortable reading desks and lounge chairs are there for the general amusement of the bored student. But that is not the total picture.

From a research and scholarly point of view, there is no such thing as serious research or scholarship in the absence of the periodical literature. Furthermore, there are profoundly important differences between the various kinds of periodical materials subscribed to by the library. To call a scholarly journal a "magazine" is a great disservice. The scholarly journal consists of heavily researched articles of a specialized nature and is published for the professionals in that field.

Magazines, on the other hand, are written for the general public, the casual reader, and are not research scholarship. Good magazine articles may be helpful in orienting the layman and the beginning researcher to the general range and nature of a topic but would never constitute the literature foundation for a serious research project. Any serious researcher would never refer to research scholarship in the journals as "magazine" articles. Language and terminology, as always, reflect the depth of the researcher's training and awareness.

The library does more than just provide copies of the latest issues of scholarly journals. It also collects the back issues and gathers them into a special collection often held in some large chamber of the library. The periodicals, therefore, are naturally divided into two categories, often called the current periodicals section or room and the bound periodicals section or room. Let us discuss them in that order.

Current periodicals. This section of the library is easily identified, for here the journals, magazines, and periodical materials to which the library subscribes may be displayed on easy-to-get-at shelves or racks arranged so that the general reader can peruse the collection, often without having to handle each item, by reading the covers of the journals where the contents may be listed in a convenient quick-to-use manner.

The current periodicals constitute the latest issues of a journal to which the library subscribes. The informed researcher will make it a frequent practice to scan all of the periodicals subscribed to by the library in his or her own field of study and interest. By merely reading the table of contents (often printed on the cover) of the major periodicals in the field, the researcher can keep up with the general development of ideas and activities of special personal interest.

As the current issue of a periodical is replaced by a later one, the older issue is usually placed somewhere near the latest one. Many shelves are arranged so that the older issues are kept immediately behind or under the current one. The researcher can locate them simply by lifting the shelf. These issues are kept together until a volume is accumulated and then sent off for binding and relocation in the Bound Periodicals Section. (A volume may constitute a year's worth of journals or perhaps only two or three months' worth. The most important criterion that libraries use is keeping the bound volume of manageable size.)

Bound periodicals. There is usually not enough room for the library to keep every issue of every journal to which it subscribes all together in the Current Periodicals Section, especially when one considers that there are often several hundred subscriptions and an accumulation of many decades. Therefore, for easy access it becomes necessary for the library to store the back issues of the major periodicals of the collection.

Virtually every library keeps some kind of list of its periodicals holdings. This list (which may take the form of a printed or computerized list, a card or book catalog, or a visible file) is an alphabetical listing of all the periodicals owned by the library and, just as importantly, the date the subscription commenced (and ended, if the journal is no longer received). Some collections could go back a hundred years, while others will date much more recently. This information is crucial, for it tells the researcher immediately whether or not a particular periodical is available in the library and at what point the subscription began (and ended).

In addition, the holdings list will tell in what form the back issues are kept. There is no use looking on the shelves if the issues are kept only in microform. Microform may be microfilm or microfiche. Some libraries may use film, while others will use fiche, and some use both. It is extremely important that the researcher know in which form the issues are kept, for that information will determine where they are located. Though sometimes located on the shelves with the bound materials, microfilm and microfiche are usually filed in special cabinets and may be kept in a special area of the library. Because of differences in shape and size, film and fiche are usually kept in separate cabinets.

Let us illustrate the importance of this listing. Say a researcher has found, through the utilization of **Religion Index One**, an excellent-sounding article on a topic of special research interest. Indexes are generic; that is, they index articles in their area of specialization without regard to the holdings of a particular library. Just because the researcher finds an entry in the index for an article does not mean that his library owns the journal that carries that article. Many steps and much time will be saved if the researcher will check the holdings list to see if the library actually subscribes to the periodical in question and, equally important, if the subscription includes the date of the sought-after article. Without the information provided in the holdings list, the researcher is destined to waste much time scurrying up and down the aisles of the Bound Periodicals Section looking for treasure that may not even be there.

The Bound Periodicals Section may be alphabetized or classified by subject, depending upon the practice of the particular library. Some libraries may not shelve bound periodicals by themselves but interfile them on the shelves with the books.

In most United States libraries, bound periodicals stacks are open to the patron so that the researcher is allowed to search out the needed journal issue independently. In some libraries, however, the stacks are closed and the researcher must request that the journals be brought to him.

Though we will discuss this point later, it should be emphasized here that the researcher must write down legibly the complete bibliographic information before beginning the search for needed materials. Frustration compounds confusion when the researcher must return again and again to the original reference in the index to get yet more information about the notation that should have been written down in its entirety at the outset.

The sad truth is that some researchers have only the faintest idea of what the Bound Periodicals Section is or how to use it. It constitutes yet another great gray bog of mystery and superstition and, therefore, is infrequently used, particularly by the undergraduate. Too often researchers presume on the basis of a quick perusal of only a few current periodicals in the Current Periodicals Section, or, even worse, a casual glance through the library catalog, that the library has nothing on the subject under consideration.

The Bound Periodicals Section of the library constitutes a secret treasury that can be opened only through the use of the indexes; but once the key is discovered, namely, how to use the indexes, that great treasury willingly offers up its holdings to the earnest researcher.

Reading a periodical. Unfortunately, inexperienced researchers too often pass over some of the added attractions in the periodical literature. In addition to finding the especially applicable article in the scholarly journal, the observant researcher will find even more. First, in some scholarly journals, the articles are preceded by a substantial and very helpful "abstract," a paragraph, often in bold or italic type, that summarizes the contents of the article. The abstract will indicate immediately to the researcher whether this particular article is going to be of value. Often the title is not exactly descriptive of the content, but the abstract most definitely is. By reading the abstract, the researcher may save valuable time.

Furthermore, if a researcher is attempting to develop a topic by first preparing a research bibliography, there is no more effective device than finding a crucial article in the periodical literature, turning to its conclusion and finding there a well-developed bibliography already prepared by the scholar who wrote the article. Often, two or three such articles will turn up more bibliographical citations than a researcher can handle for a single research project. Otherwise, a researcher might spend hours wandering the aisles of the library "hoping" to find a bibliography on the topic at hand, never realizing that such bibliographies are there if he or she only knew where to look.

Indexes

Where the researcher should look is in the periodicals indexes—an indispensable category of reference works for the researcher of religion and theology. Rather than spending hours browsing through journals at random—or even making "educated guesses"—in order to find material on the needed topic, the skilled researcher will turn to these indexes, which categorize articles and arrange them by subject. Although too numerous for a complete list here, we will give a brief description of the ones most valuable to the researcher of religion and theology. We will include a sample entry for several of them in the illustrations. Some of them index periodicals and journals, and others index other reference books. There are several basic indexes every researcher should know, most of which can be found in any library.

Many of these indexes are available in both paper and electronic format. Some contain citations only or citations plus abstracts, while others contain the full text of the original article. The scholar will want to inquire which indexes the library has and in which format.

Because things change quickly in this area, no attempt is made here to be inclusive. As H.W. Wilson Company publishes many of these indexes, the researcher may want to check the Wilson Web site at **http://www.hwwilson.com** for the latest information on a particular index and its content.

Bibliographic Index provides students and researchers with a useful tool to aid them in selecting information for their projects. It is a subject index to bibliographies in English and foreign languages, which are found in current books, pamphlets, or periodicals. The *Bibliographic Index* covers most areas in which bibliographies are compiled and offers an indication of recent scholarship and new developments in many fields. Some 50,000 monographs (books) and 2,800 periodicals are examined annually for material to be included in the index. To be listed, a bibliography must contain more than 50 citations. Sample entries are shown in Figure 4.1.

---

164   **BIBLIOGRAPHIC INDEX**

Reptiles—*cont.*
    Central America
  Campbell, Jonathan A. Amphibians and reptiles of Northern Guatemala, the Yucatán, and Belize. (Animal natural history series, v4) University of Okla. Press 1998 p345-65
    Indonesia
  Das, Indraneil. Herpetological bibliography of Indonesia. Krieger 1998 92p
Republic of Bosnia and Herzegovina *See* Bosnia and Herzegovina
Republic of the Ivory Coast *See* Ivory Coast
République de CÔte d'Ivoire *See* Ivory Coast
République Populaire du Bénin *See* Benin
Requests for proposals (Public contracts)
  Wilkinson, Frances C., and Thorson, Connie Capers. The RFP process; effective management of the acquisition of library materials. Libraries. Unlimited 1998 p181-9

Respirators *See* Breathing apparatus
Respirators (Protective equipment) *See* Breathing apparatus
Respiratory protective devices *See* Breathing apparatus
Response, Conditioned *See* Conditioned response
Responsibility
  Bok, Hilary. Freedom and responsibility. Princeton Univ. Press 1998 p215-20
  Relational responsibility; resources for sustainable dialogue; [by] Sheila McNamee [et al.] Sage Publs. 1998 p219-26
Responsibility, Criminal *See* Criminal liability
Restoration of buildings *See* Architecture—Conservation and restoration
Restore Democracy, Operation, Haiti, 1994-1995 *See* Haiti–History—American intervention, 1994-1995
Retail advertising *See* Advertising
Retail marketing *See* Marketing
Retail trade

Figure 4.1   Sample entries from *Bibliographic Index*

Biography Index is a guide to the location of biographical materials found in the books, pamphlets, and more than 3,000 periodicals appearing in other Wilson indexes. Access to all types of biographical writing from both primary and secondary sources is provided. These include autobiographies, bibliographies, critical studies, literature, letters, memoirs, pictorial works, and poetry. Some 2,000 books of individual and collective biographies are added annually. Approximately 1,600 records are added monthly. The obituaries in *The New York Times* are regularly included. Incidental materials that are found in prefaces, chapters, and bibliographies of otherwise nonbiographical works are considered important sources. *Biography Index* consists of a main alphabetical entry by last name of the subject, with a cross-reference index by profession. The index contains a checklist of composite books analyzed.

Portraits and other illustrations are noted. Entries include a wide variety of people from antiquity to the present and are chosen from all fields and nationalities. The index is updated quarterly (see Figures 4.2.A and 4.2.B).

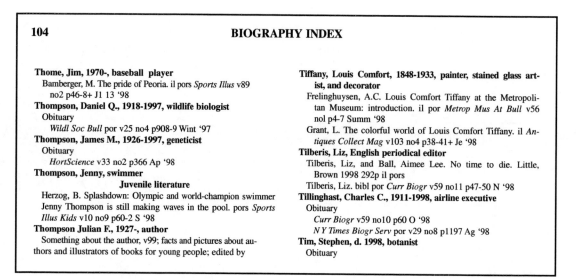

104   **BIOGRAPHY INDEX**

Thorne, Jim, 1970-, baseball player
Bamberger, M. The pride of Peoria. il pors *Sports Illus* v89 no2 p46-8+ Jl 13 '98
Thompson, Daniel Q., 1918-1997, wildlife biologist
Obituary
Wildl Soc Bull por v25 no4 p908-9 Wint '97
Thompson, James M., 1926-1997, geneticist
Obituary
HortScience v33 no2 p366 Ap '98
Thompson, Jenny, swimmer
          Juvenile literature
Herzog, B. Splashdown: Olympic and world-champion swimmer Jenny Thompson is still making waves in the pool. pors *Sports Illus Kids* v10 no9 p60-2 S '98
Thompson Julian F., 1927-, author
Something about the author, v99; facts and pictures about authors and illustrators of books for young people; edited by

Tiffany, Louis Comfort, 1848-1933, painter, stained glass artist, and decorator
Frelinghuysen, A.C. Louis Comfort Tiffany at the Metropolitan Museum: introduction. il por *Metrop Mus At Bull* v56 no1 p4-7 Summ '98
Grant, L. The colorful world of Louis Comfort Tiffany. il *Antiques Collect Mag* v103 no4 p38-41+ Je '98
Tilberis, Liz, English periodical editor
Tilberis, Liz, and Ball, Aimee Lee. No time to die. Little, Brown 1998 292p il pors
Tilberis, Liz. bibl por *Curr Biogr* v59 no11 p47-50 N '98
Tillinghast, Charles C., 1911-1998, airline executive
Obituary
Curr Biogr v59 no10 p60 O '98
N Y Times Biogr Serv por v29 no8 p1197 Ag '98
Tim, Stephen, d. 1998, botanist
Obituary

Figure 4.2.A   Sample entries from *Biography Index*

176   **INDEX TO PROFESSIONS AND OCCUPATIONS**

Rugby football players
Lomu, Jonah, 1975-
Rulers *See* Kings and rulers
Runners
Alderman, Frederick, d. 1998
Byers, Tom
Carroll, Noel, d. 1998
Cimino, Meg
Cimons, Marlene, 1945-
Clas, Brian
Drossin, Deena
Garcia, Mandy
Goucher, Adam
Hass, John R.
Hickman, Libbie
Jacobs, Regina
Maynard, Lee

Mulry, Thomas M., d. 1998
Phinn, Gervase
Ray, Henry William, 1909-
School board members
Siegel, Harold, d. 1998
School counselors *See* Student counselors
School principals
Andrus, Ethel Percy, 1884-1967
Angel, Moses, 1819-1898
Clapp, Elise Ripley, 1882-1965
Clapp, Hannah Kezia, 1824-1908
Clark, Joe
Cooke, Flora Juliette, 1864-1953
Dixon, Margaret A.
Fein, Milton
Frazier, Maude, 1881-1963
Hinton, Carmelita Chase. 1890-1983

Figure 4.2.B   Sample entries from the Index to Professions and Occupations in *Biography Index*

Book Review Digest cites and provides short excerpts of reviews of current English-language fiction and nonfiction books from approximately ninety American, British, and

Canadian periodicals. Reviews are added for approximately 600 books of adult and juvenile fiction and nonfiction in the humanities, social sciences, and general sciences each month. To qualify for inclusion, a book must have been either published or distributed in the United States or Canada. Each book is listed alphabetically in *Book Review Digest* by main entry, usually the author. Title, bibliographical information, descriptive information, review excerpts, and citations follow. This main section is followed by a subject and title index. The print version has quarterly cumulations and a permanent, bound annual cumulation. The online version is updated monthly. The inclusion of excerpts from reviews often provides the needed information without making it necessary for the researcher to locate the actual review itself. Reviews of textbooks, government publications, and technical books in the law and sciences are excluded. Figure 4.3.A shows examples of reviews and Figure 4.3.B (see page 36) shows sample index entries.

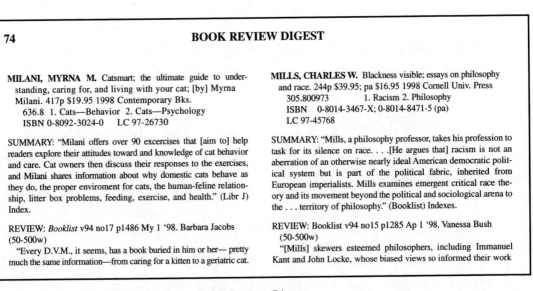

74 **BOOK REVIEW DIGEST**

MILANI, MYRNA M. Catsmart; the ultimate guide to understanding, caring for, and living with your cat; [by] Myrna Milani. 417p $19.95 1998 Contemporary Bks.
636.8 1. Cats—Behavior 2. Cats—Psychology
ISBN 0-8092-3024-0 LC 97-26730

SUMMARY: "Milani offers over 90 excercises that [aim to] help readers explore their attitudes toward and knowledge of cat behavior and care. Cat owners then discuss their responses to the exercises, and Milani shares information about why domestic cats behave as they do, the proper enviroment for cats, the human-feline relationship, litter box problems, feeding, exercise, and health." (Libr J) Index.

REVIEW: *Booklist* v94 no17 p1486 My 1 '98. Barbara Jacobs
(50-500w)
"Every D.V.M., it seems, has a book buried in him or her— pretty much the same information—from caring for a kitten to a geriatric cat.

MILLS, CHARLES W. Blackness visible; essays on philosophy and race. 244p $39.95; pa $16.95 1998 Cornell Univ. Press
305.800973 1. Racism 2. Philosophy
ISBN 0-8014-3467-X; 0-8014-8471-5 (pa)
LC 97-45768

SUMMARY: "Mills, a philosophy professor, takes his profession to task for its silence on race. . . .[He argues that] racism is not an aberration of an otherwise nearly ideal American democratic political system but is part of the political fabric, inherited from European imperialists. Mills examines emergent critical race theory and its movement beyond the political and sociological arena to the . . . territory of philosophy." (Booklist) Indexes.

REVIEW: Booklist v94 no15 p1285 Ap 1 '98. Vanessa Bush
(50-500w)
"[Mills] skewers esteemed philosophers, including Immanuel Kant and John Locke, whose biased views so informed their work

Figure 4.3.A   Sample entries from *Book Review Digest*

Book Review Index is similar in scope and purpose to **Book Review Digest**. The major difference is that *Book Review Index* gives only citations for the reviews and does not include excerpts.

Catholic Periodical and Literature Index. In 1968, the **Catholic Periodical Index** (since 1939) and **The Guide to Catholic Literature** combined to form this index. The bimonthly publication with biennial cumulations covers some 135 titles and about 2,500 books per year.

---

152   **SUBJECT AND TITLE INDEX**

Religious education
    See also
        Religion in the public schools
Religious history *See* Church history
Religious holidays
    See also
        Festivals
Religious life
    See also
        Spiritual life
Remarkable animals. Meeuwissen, T.
Renaissance, Harlem *See* Harlem Renaissance
Reporters and reporting
    See also
        Journalism
Stahl, L. Reporting live
Reporting live. Stahl, L.

Role conflict
    See also
        Sex role
Roller Coasters
                Juvenile literature
    Cook, N. Roller coasters
Roller coasters. Cook, N.
Roller skating
    See also
        In-line skating
Rollerblading *See* In-line skating
Roman Catholic Church *See* Catholic Church
Roman Empire *See* Rome
Romance literature
    See also
        French literature
Romances

Figure 4.3.B   Sample entries from the Subject and Title Index in *Book Review Digest*

Christian Periodical Index (since 1958) is an excellent companion to *Religion Index One*. Published three times a year by the Association of Christian Librarians, its purpose is to provide access to English language articles and reviews written by the evangelical community. Over 100 titles are indexed (see Figure 4.4 for a sample of the index). The index also includes a separate section containing book reviews. It is available in paper or electronic format. For further information on the *Christian Periodical Index*, see **http://www.acl.org/publications.htm**.

---

218   **CHRISTIAN PERIODICAL INDEX**

CHRISTIAN EDUCATION OF ADULTS (cont.)
Finer points of choosing instructional methods. Brad Stych. journal of Adult Training 8:17-23 no. 2 1996
Serving senior servants. Kenneth O. Gangel. Journal of Adult Training 2:10-5 no. 2 1990
Using andragogy to foster moral development of adults within the church. Eleanor Terry. Journal of Adult Training p11-6 Spr 1989
CHRISTIAN EDUCATION OF CHILDREN
Channel surfing to enhance your VBS! Judy Fondren. Evangelizing Today's Child 23:14-5 Jan 1996
The dangers of a Christian school education. Bob Moore. bibl Christian Educators Journal 37:28-9 Oct 1997
Divine revelation. Vicky Caruana. Christian Parenting Today 10:16-7 Sep 1997
A dose of courage. Mark Hammerton. ill Moody

The dangers of a Christian school education. Bob Moore. bibl Christian Educators journal 37:28-9 Oct 1997
Educating youth in South America. Kevin E. Lawson. Evangelical Missions Quarterly 32:34-42 Jan 1996
CHRISTIAN EDUCATORS—INTERVIEWS
Two careers, one marriage : Jack and Judy Balswick show how to stick together when work pulls you in opposite directions. (MP interview). Louise A. Ferrebee. ill Marriage Partnership 14:62-4+ Win 1997
CHRISTIAN ETHICS
Any ol' worldview won't do. Chuck Colson. ill port Global Church Growth Bulletin 34:1-2 Jan 1997
Broadcasting integrity : does our personal walk match our public talk? Edward Stewart. port Religious

Figure 4.4   Sample entries from the *Christian Periodical Index*

Cumulative Book Index is a current index to books published in the English language and is international in scope; 50,000 to 60,000 books are indexed each year. The index covers both fiction and nonfiction works of fifty pages or more in both hardback and paperback. There is no page limit for bibliographies, plays, poetry, juvenile literature and scholarly works. It is the only international index to list entries by author, title, and subject in a single alphabet. The author, or main, entry includes any or all of the following pertinent bibliographic information: author's or editor's name; full title of the book; illustrator's name; translator's name; indication of illustrations or maps; binding, if other than cloth; price; International Standard Book Number (ISBN), if available; publication date; publisher; edition; series note; volume number; paging; size, if other than standard shelf size; Library of Congress card number; and distributors for foreign publications available in the United States (see sample entries in Figure 4.5). Each book indexed in *Cumulative Book Index (CBI)* is cited under as many subject headings and subheadings as its contents require. Government documents, editions limited to 500 copies or fewer, inexpensive paperbound books, or materials of a local or ephemeral nature are not included. Approximately 6,000 records from all subject areas are added each month. In early 2000, H.W. Wilson announced that they were discontinuing this venerable publication after 101 years.

---

496   **CUMULATIVE BOOK INDEX**

Remnick, David
   King of the world; Muhammad Ali and the rise of an American hero. 326p il $25 (Can$35) 1998 Random House ISBN 0-375-50065-0 LC 98-24539
Remote sensing
Congresses
AIPR Workshop (26th: 1997: Washington, D.C.). Exploiting new image sources and sensors. 1998 SPIE
Satellite remote sensing of clouds and the atmosphere II. 1998 SPIE
Government policy
United States—International cooperation
Wagner, C.S. International agreements on cooperation in remote sensing and earth observation. pa 1998 Rand Corp.
Renaissance
Zophy, J.W. A short history of Renaissance and Reformation Europe. 2nd ed pa 1999 Prentice-Hall

Campbell, M.E. Focus: writing paragraphs and essays. 2nd ed pa 1999 Prentice-Hall
Elbow, P. Writing with power. 2nd ed 1998 Oxford Univ. Press
Fulwiler, T. The working writer. 2nd ed 1999 Prentice-Hall
Meiser, M.J. Good writing! 2nd ed pa 1998 Allyn & Bacon
Rooks, G. Share your paragraph. 2nd ed 1999 Prentice-Hall Regents
Handbooks, manuals, etc.
Axelrod, R.B.A. A writer's guidebook. 1998 St. Martin's Press
Juvenile literature
James, E. How to write super school reports. rev ed 1998 Lothrop, Lee & Shepard Bks.
Problems, exercises, etc.
Controversy. 1999 Prentice-Hall
Fergenson, L. All in one. 4th ed 1999 Prentice-Hall
McMahan, E. Literature and the writing process. 5th ed 1999

Figure 4.5   Sample entries from *Cumulative Book Index*

Current Book Review Citations (1976-1982) is an index of book reviews appearing in more than 1,200 periodicals between 1976 and 1982. It provides users with a guide to recent reviews of fiction and nonfiction books found in both book-reviewing periodicals and subject periodicals. *Current Book Review Citations* assists readers in locating critical evaluations from a wide variety of periodicals during those years. All the major fields of intellectual and scientific pursuits are encompassed: business, education, the humanities, law, the social sciences, and pure and applied sciences. Part I of *Current Book Review Citations* is the "Author Index." All book reviews are entered by the name of the author of the book reviewed. The title and the date of publication of the book are given, followed by the name of the periodical in which the review appeared with its volume number, date, and page numbers. The name of the reviewer is included if available. Part II is the "Title Index." When a title is used as the main entry, the full bibliographic information is to be found in the "Author Index" with a "see" reference from the entry in the "Title Index."

Education Index covers approximately 600 core English-language periodicals, books, and yearbooks published in the United States and elsewhere on a wide range of contemporary education issues such as multicultural education, religious education, student counseling, and information technology (see sample entries in Figure 4.6). Indexing began in June 1983 and abstracting began in June 1984, and full-text coverage is available from January 1996. Approximately 3,000 records are added each month. The full-text version contains articles from more than 130 periodicals plus citations and abstracts from additional journals. Abstracts are approximately 50 to 150 words each.

---

202   EDUCATION INDEX

Refereeing of educational literature *See* Educational literature
Reference books
    See also
  Encyclopedias
  Libraries, High school—Reference collections
    Teaching
  Architectural beginnings and building blocks [library media skills unit] R. Stach. bibl *Sch Libr Media Act Mon* v15 no7 p12-15 Mr '99
  Science [library media skills unit] bibl il *Sch Libr Media Act Mon* v15 no7 p21-3 Mr '99
Reference electrodes *See* Electrodes
Referral process
    See also
  Counseling centers—Referrals
  Comparison of students referred and not referred for special education. J. Gottlieb and S.L. Weinberg. bibl *Elem Sch J*

Reggio Emilia approach
  Parental reactions to the introduction of the Reggio Emilia approach in Head Start classrooms. C.S. McClow and C.W. Gillespie. bibl il *Early Child Educ J* v26 no2 p131-6 Wint '98
Regional educational cooperation *See* Cooperation, Educational
Regional educational research laboratories *See* Research laboratories
Regional literature *See* Local color in literature
Regionalism in literature *See* Local color in literature
Registration
    See also
  Enrollment
Regression analysis
    See also
  Multiple comparisons (Statistics)
  An introduction to logistic regression. G.J. Cizek and S.M. Fitzgerald. bibl *Meas Eval Couns Dev* v31 no4 p233-44

Figure 4.6   Sample entries from *Education Index*

Essay and General Literature Index. *The Essay and General Literature Index* cites essays and articles contained in collections of essays and miscellaneous works published in the United States, Great Britain, and Canada (see Figure 4.7). More than 300 volumes are indexed each year, as well as more than 20 annuals and serial publications. Approximately 4,000 records are added annually. The focus is on the humanities and social sciences.

---

160   **ESSAY AND GENERAL LITERATURE INDEX**

Robinson, Lillian S.—In the canon's mouth—
Contents—*Continued*
    I, too, am America
    In the canon's mouth
    Is there class in this text?: on The Norton
        anthology of literature by women
    The practice of theories: an immodest pro-
        posal
    The queen's necklace
    Their canon, our arsenal
    Treason our text: feminist challenges to the
        literary canon
    Waving the flag at racism and sexism: the
        semiotics and politics of "political correct-
        ness"
    What culture should mean
Robots in literature

Rogers, B. Ann, and Schott, Linda, 1957-
    "My mother was a mover": (*In* Writing the
    range; ed. by E. Jameson and S. H. Armitage
    p585-99)
Roman architecture *See* Architecture, Roman
Roman Catholic Church *See* Catholic Church
Roman de la Rose
    Blumenfeld-Kosinski, R. The myths of the Ro-
    man de la Rose. (*In* Blumenfeld-Kosinski, R.
    Reading myth p52-89)
Roman Empire *See* Rome
Romance of the Rose *See* Roman de la Rose
Romance philology
    Scaglione, A.D. Celso Cittadini and the ori-
    gins of Romance philology. (*In* Scaglione, A.D.
    Essays on the arts of discourse p343-52)
Romances

Figure 4.7   Sample entries from *Essay and General Literature Index*

General Science Index covers some 200 popular and professional English-language science periodicals (see sample entries in Figure 4.8 on page 40). Also included is the "Science" section of *The New York Times*. Citations extend back to May 1984, and abstracts date from March 1993 to the present. Approximately forty periodicals are covered in full text since January 1995. Approximately 5,000 records are added monthly.

The Guide to Social Science and Religion in Periodical Literature, published since 1965 by the National Periodical Library of Flint, Michigan, regularly scans over 100 journals for references to the social sciences and religion and contains numerous entries for occasional articles found in other journals. The publication appears biennially. The entries are arranged in an alphabetical manner by subject, similar to that which is found in *Readers' Guide* and other basic indexes. For the years 1965-1968, the title was *Guide to Religious and Semi-Religious Periodicals*.

Humanities Index. This H.W. Wilson index covers approximately 400 English-language periodicals in the humanities. Among the disciplines included are literature and language, history, philosophy, archaeology, classical studies, folklore, and religion and theology (see Figure 4.9). Indexing covers back to 1984 and abstracts are from March 1994 to date. More than 95 periodicals are covered in full text from January 1995 to date. Over 3,000 entries are added monthly, and abstracts range from approximately 50 to 150 words each.

---

202   **GENERAL SCIENCE INDEX**

Reptiles
    See also
    Crocodiles
    Komodo dragons
    Lizards
    Snakes
    Turtles
    See also subhead Reptiles under the following subjects
Competition (Biology)
Developmental genetics
Evolution
Growth
Phylogeny
Thermoregulation (Physiology)
Variation (Biology)
         Eggs
Effects of ultraviolet radiation on amphibians: field experi-

Resinous products
    See also
    Melamine
    Polyethylene
    Styrene
Amalgam vs. composite resin: 1998. G. J. Christiansen. bibl *J Am Dent Assoc* v129 no12 p1757-9 D '98
        Ion exchange
Genesis of selectivity and reversibility for sorption of synthetic aromatic anions onto polymeric sorbents. P. Li and A.K. Sengupta. bibl il *Environ Sci Technol* v32 no23 p3756-66 D 1 '98
Resistance of bacteria to antibiotics *See* Bacteria—Resistance and sensitivity
Resistance of fungi to antibiotics *See* Fungi—Resistance and sensitivity
Resistance to disease *See* Immunity

Figure 4.8   Sample entries from *General Science Index*

---

331   **HUMANITIES INDEX**

Religious liberty *See* Freedom of religion
Religious life
    See also
    Monastic life
    Spiritual life
    See also subhead Religious life under the following subjects
    Authors
    Blacks
    Blacks—South Africa
    Gays
    Men
    Mexican Americans
    Women
        Buddhism
The hard-to-please Buddhist and the 'What's it?' tree. T. Gomes. *Middle Way* v73 no3 p167-9 N '98

Religious rites *See* Rites and ceremonies
Religious societies
    See also
    Call to Renewal (Organization)
Religious Society of Friends *See* Society of Friends
Religious syncretism *See* Syncretism (Religion)
Religious thought
    See also
    Apologetics
    Good and evil
    Man (Theology)
Religious tolerance
    Lactantius, Porphyry, and the debate over religious toleration. E. D. Digeser. *J Roman Stud* v88 p129-46 '98
Rembrandt Harmenszoon van Rijn, 1606-1669
    about
    The fountain of Narcissus: the invention of subjectivity and the

Figure 4.9   Sample entries from *Humanities Index*

Index to U. S. Government Periodicals (1970-1987) provides a subject and author approach to 120 periodicals issued by various agencies of the federal government.

Published quarterly from 1970 to 1987, it is particularly useful for the social sciences for those years and, for an extensive search, should be used with *PAIS* (to be discussed below) and the *Social Science Index*.

New Testament Abstracts (since 1956) is published three times a year by the Weston School of Theology of Cambridge, Massachusetts, in conjunction with the Catholic Biblical Association of America. It indexes over 325 journals published in many languages. Abstracts are numbered within each issue, and the year-end issue contains indexes to authors, Scripture passages and book reviews.

Old Testament Abstracts (since 1978) is published three times a year by the Catholic Biblical Association of America, Catholic University of America, Washington, DC. It contains abstracts of books and articles from more than 325 periodicals that are published in many languages. Each issue is divided into broad areas by Scripture reference, with major divisions according to book types, such as the Pentateuch, historical books, major prophets, minor prophets, and the apocrypha. The year-end issue contains an index to authors and Scripture passages for the entire year. It has also been available in electronic format since 1996.

PAIS International in Print provides a selective subject listing of the latest books, pamphlets, government publications, reports of public and private agencies, and periodical articles relevant to government and public administration, international affairs, and economics. It has the advantage of relative currency since it is issued twice a month and cumulated four times a year. Retrospective searching may be accomplished through the *Cumulative Subject Index to the PAIS Annual Bulletin* (1915-1974). An example is provided in Figure 4.10. In addition, *PAIS* has been online since 1976.

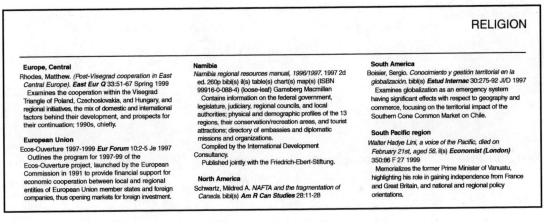

Figure 4.10   Sample entries from *PAIS International in Print*

Readers' Guide to Periodical Literature. This old standby from high school days is still useful to the university student and researcher of religious studies. Public libraries, which are often the only libraries available to practicing clergy, may not have many of the previously mentioned titles, but most will have *RG*. Aimed at the general public, *RG* covers a broad spectrum of journals, including several titles of interest to clergy such as *Christian Century, America, Commonweal,* and *Christianity Today*—some 250 titles altogether. Articles are indexed by author and subject, with entries for both located in a single alphabet. Each author and subject entry includes all the necessary bibliographic information to find the article cited: author's name, title of the article, title of the periodical, volume number, inclusive paging of the article, date of publication, and notations of illustrations, bibliographies, or other descriptive information. Book reviews are cited in a separate section. Approximately 7,000 items are added monthly. *RG* is issued monthly in print with annual cumulations. The print version dates back to 1900. Sample entries are shown in Figure 4.11. The electronic version dates to January 1983 and includes abstracts since September 1984. Full text has been included since January 1994.

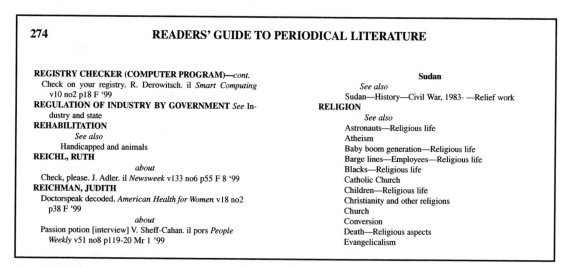

Figure 4.11   Sample entries from *Readers' Guide to Periodical Literature*

Religion Index One: Periodicals has been around since 1949. Published semiannually with biennial cumulations, it was formerly called ***Index to Religious Periodical Literature*** (1949-1976). It indexes religious and archaeological journals from the United States, Canada, England, Scotland, Germany, Japan, France, and several other countries. It currently indexes some 380 periodicals (see Figure 4.12). While its focus is primarily Protestant, it also includes some Catholic and Jewish titles. It indexes articles by subject and author and contains abstracts. There is a separate index for book reviews. It is also available in electronic format.

Refugees, African	334	Subject Index

Refugees, African
1998 Maputo Consultation for a More Co-ordinated Pastoral Response to the Refugee Crisis in Africa: Final Statement—29 January 1998. *SEDOS* 30:126-127 Ap 1998

Refugees, Cuban
see also Alexander, Nobel
Cuba's Next Revolution: how Christians are reshaping Castro's Communist stronghold [maps, photos]. Kennedy, John W. *Chr T* 42:18-25 Ja 12 1998
Religious Community in a Cuban Refugee Camp: Bringing Order Out of Chaos [bibliog, table]. Payne, William P. *Missiology* 25:133-154 Ap 1997

Refugees, Jewish
Foreigners or Jews? The Soviet Jewish Refugee Populations in Germany and the United States [tables]. Tress, Madeleine. *E Europe Jew Affairs* 27:21-38 Wint 1997

Refugees, Religious
German "Non-Aryan" Clergymen and the Anguish of Exile After 1933 [appendix]. Webster, Ronald D E. *J Rel Hist* 22:83-103 F 1998

Reinhardt, Rudolf
Die Reichskirche in der Neuzeit: Rudolf Reinhardts Beitrag zu ihrer Etforschung [paper presented at Stuttgart, ja 23 1998]. Weitlauff, Manfred. *Z K G* 109 no 1:2-18 1998

Reiteration *see* Repetition

Relation (Philosophy)
Relational Personalism [bibliog; reply, J Padgett, pp 43-52]. Oliver, Harold H. *Person Forum* 5:27-42 Spr 1989

Relation (Theology)
Memoirs and Witnessings ["personal accounts of theological events and/or relationships"]. Lytle, Guy F, ed. *Sewanee Th R* 40:263-356 Pentecost 1997*

Relativity
Can Hartshorne Escape Dharmakirti? Some Reflections with Implications

Figure 4.12   Sample entries from *Religion Index One*

Religious and Theological Abstracts (since 1958) indexes journal articles and includes brief abstracts. Published quarterly by Religious and Theological Abstracts, Inc., a nonsectarian abstracting service, it includes Christian, Jewish, and Muslim titles. Articles are classed into four major areas: Biblical, theological, historical, and practical. The fourth issue of the year indexes all issues by subject, author, and Scripture reference.

Social Sciences Index, like many other Wilson indexes, comes in index, abstract, and full-text formats. It covers over 400 English-language periodicals on topics such as anthropology, area studies, criminal justice, economics, international relations, political science, psychiatry, psychology, social work, and urban studies. Index coverage dates from February 1983, and abstracts are available back to January 1994. Full-text coverage of over 100 periodicals began in January 1995. Approximately 4,000 records are added each month, and abstracts run from 50 to 150 words each (see Figure 4.13 on page 44).

Vertical File Index from H.W. Wilson is a guide to pamphlets from many public and private sources, including businesses; federal, state, and local governments; not-for-profit organizations; think tanks; and small presses. The print version is updated monthly.

---

783   SOCIAL SCIENCES INDEX

Religious liberty—*cont.*
                              China
Among the flock: faith springs eternal in remote Sichuan. M.
  Forney. il *Far East Econ Rev* v161 no27 p29+ Jl 2 '98
Blind faith [religious persecution in China and U.S. Christians]
  D. Lutterbeck. il *Far East Econ Rev* v161 no27 p28-9 Jl 2
  '98
Zhu Rongji speaks on religious, financial and economic issues.
  Beijing Rev v41 no38 p5 S 21 '98
Religious life *See* Church membership; Faith
Religious literature
Religion and politics and Sub-Saharan Africa. S. Ellis and G.
  ter Haar. *J Mod Afr Stud* v36 no2 p175-201 Je '98
Religious movements
            See also
        Cargo movement
        Church renewal

Attachment styles, reminiscence functions, and happiness in
  young and elderly adults. J. D. Webster. bibl *J Aging Stud*
  v12 no3 p315-30 Fall '98
Remittances, Emigrant *See* Emigrant remittances
Remmel, Robert
  Project HAPPEN: where law enforcement and housing code
    enforcement meet. *Am J Public Health* v88 no6 p978-9 Je
    '98
Remodeling of buildings for other use *See* Buildings—Remod-
  eling for other use
Remote control
            See also
        Guided missiles
        Television receivers—Control
Remote control flipping, Television *See* Grazing (Television
  viewing)
Remote sensing

Figure 4.13   Sample entries from *Social Sciences Index*

Several of the previously mentioned indexes, and many others, are now available online. An increasing number of them are becoming available as CD-ROM products or via the World Wide Web and are more likely than ever to be found even in smaller libraries. Ask which ones are available at your library or nearby libraries.

In addition to the previously mentioned indexes, some libraries subscribe to online services through one of several subscription services. Before beginning online research through one of the vendors, the researcher should understand something about how charges are incurred, as searching online can be quite expensive. (See Chapter Five for more detail on how these charges are calculated.)

Before you are scared off by the thought of paying hundreds of dollars to find a few articles, remember that the librarian is skilled at performing this type of search—some librarians more than others—so make sure you choose one who is skilled. An expert searcher can conduct a search and produce a list of relevant articles in just a few seconds or minutes. (Two minutes spent in a $300 per hour database is only $10.)

It is for this reason that the librarian will often ask you to fill out one or more forms outlining your search and the desired results as carefully as possible. He or she will often ask you the maximum you want to spend and the number of citations you want to retrieve.

The reason for an online search is that it may be tailored to your needs much more exactly than a manual search. For example, you may be interested only in research that was published in the German language between 1983 and 1985. An online search will allow you to retrieve that type of information specifically. If, for example, you have already done a lot of research and do not need any of the articles written by John Doe, you may exclude them from your search. Or you (viz. the searcher) may program the computer to advise you each month if anything new is published in your area of interest. (This service is called SDI—Selective Dissemination of Information.)

Some of the databases of specific interest to the researcher of religion that are now available online are the Bible (various versions), the ***Philosopher's Index***, and ***Religion Index***. Many of the other hundreds of available databases may also contain articles of interest to the religion student, seminarian, or pastor. Online searching is an extremely useful tool for the professional researcher. Everyone should at least be introduced to it.

Those who learn to use periodicals indexes early in their career and to use them well will find that it makes their research easier, and gives it a timeliness lacking in that of many of their colleagues.

Chapter Five

Electronic Resources and the Internet

"...The Good, the Bad, and the Ugly..."

The very first issue that must be dealt with while facing the world of electronic information is the issue of finding the *best* of all possible sources. Some researchers, particularly younger ones, exhibit a strong tendency to want to find everything in electronic format. Other users are especially resistant to anything that is not printed on paper. Good research lies at neither of those two extremes. What the excellent researcher *must* find is the *best* source of information to meet his or her needs, regardless of the format. Depending on the nature of the query, both electronic and paper sources may be roughly equal, or one may be far superior to the other.

For example, a researcher who is already in the library and needs to know the population of the world may find it much more quickly by approaching the reference librarian and asking the straightforward question, "What is the current world population?" In all likelihood, the reference librarian will quickly grab the latest edition of *World Almanac* from a shelf within arm's reach and have the figure in less than a minute—far faster than poking around on the World Wide Web, trying to locate a site that *might* have the information, and then locating the information itself. Even from home or the office, the researcher might find it quicker to call the telephone reference service at the library and ask the question than to try to find it online.

On the other hand, if he needs the latest, most up-to-the-minute information, it is far more likely to be current in an online source such as the world population clock **<http://metalab. unc.edu/lunarbin/worldpop>** or **<http://www.census.gov/cgi-bin/ipc/popclockw>** than in a print publication. It may be much better to use the online information even if it takes a while to determine that such a site exists and to discover its location.

Format has no bearing on the quality of information; no source is inherently better than another because of its format—though one may be easier to use, more current or more precise in locating the desired information than the other because of the usability its format provides. If the scholar is unsure whether a print or an online source would be the better choice, ask the person trained in locating and evaluating reference sources—the reference librarian.

Today's highly connected world is replete with electronic resources of all kinds. All these resources can be categorized into one of only two kinds: good ones and bad ones. Electronic resources need to be evaluated against the same criteria discussed in Chapter Three under "Evaluating a Reference Book."

One of the main problems—and benefits—of the World Wide Web is that virtually anyone can mount Web pages and become an information provider. There is no control over who mounts the information, and no editing to keep the information correct and well-written.

Just as with a print source, the student should always ask the following questions:

- Who is the author of this information?

- Is he or she a reliable source?

- Is he or she an authority in the field?

- Who is the publisher? The fact that the information is mounted on a university server somewhere does not necessarily make it reliable; it could be information mounted on the Web page of a freshman student. Does the university endorse the information?

- What is the purpose of this information? Did the author mount the information as part of his or her scholarly research? Or was it mounted as part of her job? Did he mount the information in order to convince the world of his own point of view on a topic, regardless of the facts?

- Is the information current? When was it created or last updated? When is it likely to change again?

- In those cases where currency is important, how old is the information?

- Does the author show bias toward or against the subject? In today's world, it is all too common for individuals to mount an attack against another person or company. This attack may be open or sometimes hidden under the guise of "scholarly information."

- Is the information copyrighted? Original works of scholarship are considered property of their author and are protected under copyright law regardless of whether they bear notice of copyright or not—unless the author has explicitly stated that the work has been placed in the public domain. Even so, the scholar must make sure that the person saying he has placed the work in the public domain is its sole owner and is entitled to do so. With electronic resources, it is far too easy to cut-and-paste information into a research paper without proper citation or acknowledgement of copyright.

- Is the work indexed? Perhaps an index is not quite so important in an electronic work as in a paper one because the scholar can often use a "find" or "search" function to locate the needed information. But the information needs to be organized well enough to be useful without wasting a lot of the researcher's time.

- How is the material organized? It is just as important for material to be logically organized in an electronic resource as in a print one, even though the limitation of poor organization may be easier to overcome in an electronic environment.

Another major problem with electronic resources, particularly those mounted on the Internet and the World Wide Web, is that they may disappear quickly. It seems to be fairly common, for example, for a given university to maintain a Web site on a certain topic with reliable scholarly, authoritative information for several years. Then, the student who was maintaining the site graduates or the professor gets a new job, and the information ceases to be updated or disappears altogether.

Good Sources of Information

The serious researcher quickly discovers that the Internet is full of unreliable sources of questionable information. Are there any good sources out there? If so, what are some of them?

The Internet was created by the United States government for military purposes. It was quickly embraced by the academic and scholarly community as a way for researchers to share information quickly and efficiently. Only in the late 1990s, after the creation of the World Wide Web and as online tools became easier to use, did the Internet begin to be dominated by the commercial sector. The government and scholarly sources of information have not disappeared; they have just become harder to find in a very crowded world.

Always note the domain name of a site. ".com" usually indicates a commercial site; ".org" an organization, often not-for-profit; ".net" indicates a network of some type; and ".edu" is a United States institution of higher education. Two other domain types are ".gov" for sites belonging to the United States federal government and ".mil" for the

United States military. The domain name can be a big clue as to the purpose of a Web site and a key to the type of information you can expect to find there.

It should be noted that the presence of a tilde character, "~", in the URL may be a significant clue to the validity of a Web site. The presence of a tilde in an address such as "www.harvard.edu/~jones" may indicate that the page is maintained by a student or a faculty member named "Jones." In other words, the presence of ".edu" in a URL does not automatically indicate that the pages being viewed are authorized and/or maintained by the university.

Here are some of the more reliable types of sources.

Colleges and Universities

One of the best sources of information for the researcher is the college or university that conducts research in or specializes in a given discipline. Just as we might expect, one would not be disappointed by looking to the Harvard Business School, **http://www.hbs.harvard.edu/**, for business information or the Harvard Divinity School, **http://divweb.harvard.edu/**, for information in the area of religion and theology. Among other resources, the publications of these two schools, found in whole or in part on their Web site, *Harvard Business Review, Harvard Divinity Bulletin, Harvard Theological Review,* and *Religion & Value in Public Life,* can provide much information in their respective areas.

Colleges and universities that teach a particular discipline have often created a Web site with links to many useful resources in that discipline for their students. These sites are generally open to nonstudents as well. Thus, if one knows that a school offers degrees in a certain field, he can look there as a starting point to find related resources rather than blindly searching the Web.

Obviously, many church-affiliated colleges and universities will offer majors in subject areas of interest to the student and scholar in religion and theology. Many of these sites provide excellent research materials, as well as links to other useful resources. A listing of the members of the **Council for Christian Colleges & Universities** can be seen at **http://www.gospelcom.net/cccu/**. Each listing entry is an active hotlink to the college or university.

Government Sources

Governments gather data and create information. Because it is paid for with tax dollars, much of this information is in the public domain. Governments at all levels (city, state, federal, etc.) in many countries are now realizing that it may be less expensive for them to provide this information over the Internet than to produce multiple copies of large documents in a print version. This has created a pool of great wealth for the researcher.

The first step in using government information is for the researcher to determine which government body might have produced the information he or she needs. Which country would have produced the information? At what level would the information have been produced? At the federal level? The state or province level? The county or municipal level?

The next step is to determine *where* the information might have been produced. In the United States, for example, information about a given state is likely to have been produced by that state, not by a state on the other side of the continent.

If the researcher is not sure where to begin a search, he or she should bear in mind that many governments have linked their sites to other government sites. For example, the United States federal government has established the **Federal Information Center (FIC)** Internet site at **http://fic.info.gov/** and the **Government Information Xchange** at **http://www.info.gov/cgi-bin/search_gov**. The researcher can locate information on these sites by browsing or by using a search engine on the site to find information by keyword. At the FIC site, the researcher can find links to myriad federal government Web sites, as well as links to state and local government sites. Web sites are listed both by state and by topical subject area. In addition, some government bodies provide telephone numbers, sometimes tollfree, that the researcher can call for assistance in locating information.

Another useful site that is maintained by the United States federal government is **FedWorld** at **http://www.fedworld.gov/**. FedWorld offers a gateway to many other government information systems as well as United States government reports and access to many other federal government Web sites.

There are many other pertinent Web sites. The **United States Government Printing Office** <http://www.gpo.gov/> provides information on many topics, particularly those related to the federal government and legal matters. Both houses of the **United States Congress** maintain Web sites at **http://www.senate.gov/** and **http://www.house.gov,** respectively. Two other important and useful federal government sites are the **White House** at **http://www.whitehouse.gov/** and **Thomas**, a government information site maintained by the Library of Congress at **http://thomas.loc.gov/**.

Almost all state governments in the United States can be located with the Web address http://www.state.[postal abbreviation].us, for example, **http://www.state.ca.us/** for California or **http://www.state.tx.us/** for Texas. The abbreviation used for the state is the official postal code used by the United States Postal Service. On their sites, states have links to county and city government sites. Many states also provide links to the federal government and to other states.

There are links to the governments of many other countries, as well. For example, there are links to all United Kingdom government authorities at the **CCTA Government Information Service** Web site at **http://www.open.gov.uk/**.

Entire books have been written about United States and other government Internet sites. The researcher expecting to need to use much such information is well advised to acquire some of these.

Organizations

As the World Wide Web has grown in popularity, virtually every not-for-profit organization of any size has established a Web site. These sites provide much information freely available to all. Because of the nature of these organizations, such information is generally ample and authoritative. Examples of such groups would be the **American Cancer Society <http://www.cancer.org/>** or the **American Heart Association <http://www.americanheart.org>**.

Hobbyists, collectors, and aficionados of all types have created Web sites around their mutual interest. Such sites include the **American Numismatic Association <http://www.money.org/>** or **Collectors.Org <http://www.collectors.org>**.

Another organization type that may be of great usefulness to the scholar in religion and theology are church-affiliated sites. Many national and international church organizations have their own site, as do an increasing number of local congregations. Many mission boards and religious societies have their own Web site. Often these sites can provide valuable links to further resources. One such well-known site, the **Gospel Communications Network**, has links to many mission-related organizations at **http://www.gospelcom.net/welcome/categories/missions.shtml**.

Many professional societies now have information available online to members and non-members alike, such as the **American Medical Association <http://www.ama-assn.org/>** or the **American Psychological Association <http://www.apa.org/>**.

Libraries

Libraries are specialists in organizing information. Just as they have organized books and materials within the library for many years, many libraries are now organizing information outside the library walls by establishing Web sites with many resources useful to the researcher, particularly links to other useful sites.

The primary starting place for a researcher in the United States might well be the Library of Congress at **http://www.loc.gov/**, while the researcher in Britain might want to start with **The British Library** at **http://portico.bl.uk/**. **The National Library of Canada** can be located at **http://www.nlc-bnc.ca/**. Similarly, many other countries have their own national library. Many of these national libraries have links to other libraries, including libraries in other countries, as well as state or provincial and local libraries.

In the United States, most states have an official state library or library agency. Unfortunately, the address pattern varies from state to state, so while the State Library of Indiana can be found at **http://www.statelib.lib.in.us/**, the address for the State Library of California is not http://www.statelib.lib.ca.us/. A list of links to state libraries and agencies can be found at **http://www.dpi.state.wi.us/dpi/dlcl/pld/statelib.html**. There is also a list at **http://www.lib.de.us/libraries/otherlibs/statelib.shtml**.

Some library networks are combining their efforts to provide a suite of online databases freely available to all the residents of their particular state. A few prime examples are: **SAILOR, Maryland's Online Public Information Network <http://www.sailor.lib.md.us/>**; **ACLIN, Access Colorado Library and Information Network <http://www.aclin.org/>**; **Galileo, Georgia Library Learning Online <http://www.galileo.peachnet.edu/Homepage.cgi>**; and **INSPIRE, Indiana Spectrum of Information Resources <http://www.inspire-indiana.net/>**.

An increasing number of libraries are offering online reference services, not only to their particular constituents, but to anyone. If the researcher can wait from 24 to 48 hours for a response to a query, this may be an excellent source of information. The user enters the query online via the library's Web page and receives the answer by email. One such site is the **Internet Public Library <http://www.ipl.org/>**.

Some libraries are specialists in specific subject areas, so visiting one of those sites can lead the researcher to many other useful sites on that particular topic. Ask the reference librarian for information on good sites for specific topics.

Commercial Enterprises

Although the government, educational, and military sectors originally dominated the Internet, today one of the largest types of suppliers of information via the Internet is the commercial sector. Many of these companies offer goods and services for sale, while others offer information and wares at no charge in exchange for wading through the commercial advertisements that sponsor the site. Certainly, the scholar in theology will find useful sites such as Christian bookstores and publishers, not to mention their counterparts in the secular sector.

Among the better known bookstores on the Web are **Amazon.com <http://www. amazon.com/>**, **Borders <http://borders.com/>**, and **Barnes and Noble <http:// www.barnesandnoble.com/>**.

In addition to bookstores and publishers, almost every type of business imaginable has a presence on the World Wide Web. Without knowing the exact address of the company, it is often possible to locate the company simply by guessing that the address is probably www.company-name.com. Many of these sites are authorities in their field, offering the user much helpful information and often leading to other useful sites.

Electronic Journals

There are thousands of journals and magazines available via the World Wide Web. Like their print counterparts, these range from scholarly to general interest to limited interest. In fact, some of them seem to come and go so quickly that they are probably in a class called "no interest."

Also like their print counterparts, these electronic journals run the gamut from excellent to poor. At the top end are the scholarly journals. In some cases, these journals are exact versions of their print equivalent, while others are limited, providing only a table of contents or a few select articles.

At the bottom of the ladder are the "ezines," magazines published often for a relatively limited special-interest group. Depending on the topic and the writers, these can range from excellent to worthless and must be read while applying the same measurements for quality reference sources previously outlined.

Some of these publications, particularly the scholarly journals, may be available only via subscription, and often at a high price. A good first stop is the library, which may have purchased a subscription for its patrons.

Others are highly commercial, freely available to the reader, supported by the online ads one must view in order to read the publication. And some may be free to the user and free of commercial affiliations, perhaps because they are published by a scholarly society by and for its members, or because someone publishes them as a labor of love to support a particular interest. Quality varies widely. As may be expected, some are excellent and some are not worth the electrons they are written with.

Electronic publications may be valuable sources of information, but in today's world, they have not yet achieved the scholarly acceptance of print resources, unless they are the electronic version of the same title in print.

Electronic Journalism

Every type of journalism that we are familiar with has now migrated to the World Wide Web: magazines, newspapers, radio stations, and TV stations. Anyone who did not want to be left behind has now made the journey. Often, the sources we are already familiar with can be good sources for instant information. Need to check the weather but it is not time for the local news? Check the Web site of the local TV station. Do you know of a story that was featured in yesterday's newspaper but you didn't get to buy a copy? Check the newspaper's Web site. There is a list of newspapers, organized by location or subject at **NewsDirectory.com <http://www.ecola.com/news/>**. Want to know what time a particular show will be on television this evening? Check the Web site of the local TV station, newspaper, or perhaps even the affiliated radio station. Broadcast.com provides a list of radio and TV stations searchable by call letters, format or location at **http://www.broadcast.com/**.

Search Engines

In the early to mid-1990s, before the Internet became more commercial and moved into the public domain, there was a lot of information available from government and academic sources, but it was practically impossible to find. About the only way to find information back then was to know its location—which the researcher often did not.

As much of the Internet migrated to the World Wide Web in the mid to late 1990s, we saw the development of the search engine. These services, usually paid for by commercial advertising, and therefore free to the end user, routinely search and index many of the sites on the Internet. Basically, they can be divided into four categories:

1. General Search Engines

General search engines, as the name describes, index sites and information of all types, regardless of subject or location or language. There are numerous general search engines available on the Web, with the number changing almost daily as new search engines appear and others merge with or are bought out by the competition. A few of the general search engines are listed in the Appendix, but the researcher must bear in mind that the name and address of these resources may have changed or disappeared before this book sees print.

There are several important factors the researcher must remember about these search engines:

- Search engines run a program—often called a crawler, robot, worm or some other name—that searches the Internet daily, often a different part of the Net each day until completing its rotation and beginning again. The information these programs retrieve is placed into a database and indexed. When the user searches the Web using one of these search engines, he is really searching just the database, which has already searched the Web and retrieved some information. Because the Net is searched in segments, the information in the database may not be most up-to-date; it is simply what the crawler found the day it searched.

- The search engines retrieve and index whatever they find; no attempt is made to evaluate the quality of the sites or to differentiate between sites that are definitive and those that contain erroneous or false information.

- Not all search engines will return the same results for an identical search. There are several reasons for this:

    - Not all search engines find and index the same sites. In fact, in a 1998 study, it was determined that no single search engine indexed even as much as 50 percent of the estimated 320 million Web pages available.[1]

    - Each search engine uses its own criteria to assign index terms to the data it has placed into its database. Because the indexing is automated, it may or may not be accurate.

    - When a user performs a search for information, each search engine uses its own set of algorithms to determine the relevance of a Web document to the search terms.[2] The algorithms are based on such factors as how many times the sought-after term occurs; whether the term occurs in the title of the document, a header, or within the text; the proximity of one search term to another within the document; the number of terms from the document that match the query; and numerous other factors. Not all search engines use the same factors. In any case, each search engine places a different value on each of these factors.

    With all these variables, it is easy to see why different search engines may return different sets of documents.

- Because requests for information are interpreted and analyzed by computer software with no human intervention, search results can be only as good as an engine's retrieval algorithm. A poorly written formula will either miss important documents or return many irrelevant ones—or both.

- Not all search engines allow the same search options. For example, one search engine may allow a search to be restricted by date or language, whereas another may not, thereby leading to different results.

Finally, the researcher needs to learn something about proper searching techniques. The proper way to conduct a search is not to go to one of the general search engines and directly type in the question, such as "When is Shakespeare's birthday?" as novice searchers often do. Rather, the searcher should use the general search engine to locate Web sites dealing with the topic, in this case "Shakespeare," then search those Shakespeare-related Web sites for the desired information.

The best advice for the researcher seeking breadth and depth of information is to use more than one search engine to locate the desired information.

2. Specialized Search Engines

Another type of search engine is the specialized search engine. These search engines can be categorized by the subject matter they cover or by the type of sites they index. Usually these search engines are limited to a specific format or subject area.

- **Dejanews** <http://www.dejanews.com/> is an index to the messages posted in the various online newsgroups.

- **DevSearch** <http://www.devsearch.com/> is the first search engine created for the people who make the Web. It indexes only sites that are relevant to making Web pages.[3]

- **BusinessWeb** <http://www.businesswebsource.com/> indexes business information and advertises itself as "The Source for Business Knowledge."

Whereas the general search engine attempts to search any information that is available on the World Wide Web, the specialized search engine attempts only to locate and index resources of a given type or in a certain subject area. The result is that a specialized search engine may yield information that is more relevant to the topic and easier for the searcher to find without retrieving a lot of irrelevant information. If the researcher can locate a search engine in his or her area of interest, it can be a much better source to use than a general search engine.

3. Metasearch Engines

The difference between a metasearch engine and the general search engine is that a metasearch engine allows the user to enter the search terms once and search multiple search engines simultaneously. There are, however, a couple of important cautions in using metasearch engines:

- Some metasearch engines limit the number of documents retrieved from each search engine, often to between ten and 25 items.

- The program may time out before the search engine has had time to retrieve all the relevant documents.

- The search terms entered into the metasearch engine may not be treated the same way by each search engine. For example, terms may have been entered using a Boolean "and" in the metasearch engine but the "and" is ignored by the general search engine and the terms are "or"ed together, resulting in a great number of irrelevant documents.

In conclusion, a metasearch engine may be a good starting place or a great timesaver in a pinch, but the researcher wanting great breadth and depth of information should not rely on a metasearch engine alone.

4. Directories

Directories should not be confused with search engines, though some sites, such as Yahoo! have search capabilities as well as a directory. A directory is a site that has information arranged into hierarchical categories by subject, such as "education," "science," "social sciences," "entertainment," "travel," "news," and "weather."

Because these categories have been organized with human intervention—sometimes by librarians or information specialists—they may be quicker and easier to search and yield more precise results than a general search engine. For example, a search for "travel" on **AltaVista <http://www.altavista.com/>** yielded 29,574,298 results; a search for "'travel' and 'Oxford'" yielded 2,089,810 Web pages.[4] A search through the AltaVista directories allowed us to go from the top level through "Travel & Vacations," "Europe," "Great Britain," "Regional

England," "Central & Eastern," to various travel guides on Oxford, our destination, in only five mouse clicks.

Of course, some topics, such as "travel" and "entertainment" are popular and easy to find in the directories, whereas topics of more limited interest, such as "religious wars" may be impossible or nearly so to find through the directories. A search for "religious wars" on AltaVista yielded 3,812 items, many of them highly relevant to our topic.

Many of the problems with using search engines were well summarized by Randolph Hock:

> *Unfortunately—and the impact of this continues into the present—none of the search engines took advantage of the heavy-duty searching technology and approaches found in online services such as* Dialog *and* LEXIS-NEXIS. *Neither did the search engines nor their cousins, the Web directories, take advantage of the extensive subject classification theory and practice of the last hundred or so years.*[5]

An increasing number of the general search engines are developing a directory structure in addition to their search engine. The researcher seeking such a structure might well start by visiting the page of one of these search engines.

Much valuable background and current information about search engines can be found at **Search Engine Watch <http://www.searchenginewatch.com/>**.

Online Search Services

Online search services, like ***Dialog*** and ***LEXIS-NEXIS*** just mentioned, have been around for a number of years and, through libraries, have been available to the general public longer than the Internet and the World Wide Web. Dialog Corporation, for example, became the world's first commercial online service in 1972.

How do these online services differ from what is generally available over the Internet? There are numerous ways. First of all, these services are not free. Many of them require a subscription for a searcher to access their services, thus requiring that the researcher know in advance that he or she is going to use the services. As some of these services are quite expensive, the occasional searcher will want to access them through his or her employer or through the library. Many public, academic, and corporate libraries are subscribers to these online services.

Charges for these services are calculated based on a number of factors:

- *Subscription charge.* Sometimes there is a subscription charge just to access the service. Sometimes some or all of this charge may be considered a prepay and is credited against future use of the services. If the user is accessing the service through a library or some other entity, that organization will be the one to pay the subscription fee.

- *Telecommunications charges.* The user must pay a telecommunication charge to connect to the online service. If the access is available via the Internet, there may be no telecommunications charges or only a modest one from the vendor to offset the expense of making that type of connection available. If the user must access the service directly, this charge may appear in the form of a long distance phone call from the user's location to the location of the provider's computer.

- *Connection charges.* Sometimes there is a connection charge for accessing a particular database. Even if there is no activity, the user may be charged for the amount of time he or she is connected to the database. Therefore, it is advisable that the user be prepared to conduct the search quickly and get offline to analyze the results. As some databases are less expensive than others, the user may want to create the search in a cheaper database, save it, and then transfer it to the more expensive database. Connection charges can range all the way from a few dollars per hour to hundreds of dollars per hour.

- *Activity charges.* Some search services may levy activity charges instead of or in addition to connection charges. Activity charges are based on the database being searched and the amount of processor time used by the computer in conducting the search. A more difficult search will take more computer time and, therefore, be more expensive. Likewise, a search retrieving many items may take longer and be more expensive than one that retrieves few items.

- *Citation charges.* Users may be charged for each citation retrieved. The amount charged will vary with the type of information viewed, for example, citations only, citations with abstracts, or full text. Obviously, full text will be the more expensive option.

- *Print charges.* There may be a print charge for some citations. Again, the charges will vary depending upon the format requested. Charges will also vary depending upon the retrieval method: whether viewed online, sent via e-mail, faxed, or printed offline and sent via regular mail.

• *Local service charges.* Some organizations, such as the library, may levy a service charge to pay for maintaining the equipment, the connection, and the time and training of the person who conducts the search for the user.

Naturally, the more quickly and accurately a search can be performed, the lower the cost. The logical conclusion is that it is often most cost-effective to have a librarian or professional searcher conduct the search for the researcher.

The databases available through these services have been created and maintained by librarians and subject experts in their particular area. Therefore, the articles contained therein are most likely to be of interest to the professional researcher and may have been screened for quality and accuracy.

Web pages are generally not created to be searchable but to be viewed. Because these databases are created to be searchable and are created by professionals, the information is usually divided into fields and subfields for greater precision in information retrieval. Their search engines are specially created to take advantage of these search handles. The end result is that the retrieval of records can be more precise and quicker.

Local Databases

Many libraries may own or subscribe to databases either on a local server or on CD-ROM. Many of these databases are those that the researcher would have to pay to use if trying to access them directly or over the Internet. These databases may be accessible over the library's network or, if on CD-ROM, they may be available for checkout—both in-house and external—from the library's circulation or reference desk. Some of them may be available to the library patron from home via dialup or the Internet. Ask which ones your library has that may be of interest to you and how you can get access.

Some of these databases may be of highly local interest and available nowhere else. Some examples would be an index to the local newspaper, or at least its obituaries, or a database of flowers or birds of the state or region.

Libraries and Internet Access

As we have already mentioned, many libraries now have Internet access. This benefits the researcher in numerous ways. First of all, if the user does not have Internet access from home or the office, it is often available through the local public or university library. The resources of a library are no longer limited to those contained within its walls.

Because libraries specialize in providing information, they may likely have had other patrons performing research in your major subject area. The reference staff may know of useful Internet resources that they can point you to.

In addition, the library may have created "pathfinders" or bibliographies in various subject areas. These may be in print form containing a list of Internet sites relevant to that topic, or they may be online, permitting the user direct access to the resources via the hyperlinks contained in the document.[6]

Other Online Databases

The library or educational institution may provide its users or students with access to other databases and resources that the user would normally have to pay a subscription fee to access. The difference between these databases and those mentioned previously under "Online Search Services" is that most of these charge a flat fee rather than a per-use fee. Thus, the institution pays a specific amount for access to the resource—usually an annual fee—and users can access it as much as they want with no additional charges incurring to them or to the library.

Many of these databases are from commercial concerns such as H.W. Wilson or EBSCO. In some cases, they may be provided to the library by state and local or regional consortia. Some of the databases may have been created by the library.

Document Delivery

The purpose of a document delivery service is, as the name says, to provide documents for the researcher. In most cases, we are referring to documents that are less than book length, as book length manuscripts can be obtained using the interlibrary loan services of the researcher's library.

The suppliers are companies or organizations, often commercial, that can retrieve almost anything for a fee. A quick-and-dirty definition might be, "we can get almost anything you can pay for" although this hardly does justice to the many libraries and not-for-profit organizations that provide this service for the benefit of the researcher, seeking only to cover their costs.

A researcher may find a reference to a specific document either through his reading, on the Web, or through online searching. It may be that the desired document, such as an article in a copyrighted journal, is not freely available in electronic form. Or, perhaps the researcher is not near a library where the document might be retrieved. This is the gap that a document delivery service is meant to fill.

Some document delivery services may themselves contain search engines or subject indexes that the researcher can use to locate relevant articles. Others may not. Regardless of how the citation is discovered, it is the function of the document delivery service to produce the article for the user.

First, let us clarify a couple of points: A document delivery service does not usually provide original documents. A document delivery service would not be the place to request an original folio of Shakespeare. It may, however, be able to provide a photocopy or electronic facsimile of that folio. Essentially, document delivery services are able to provide documents that can be photocopied or scanned into electronic format, or that are already available in electronic format.

As the first step in retrieving a document, the researcher must locate an accurate citation. If the citation information is inaccurate, it is quite likely that the retrieval service will be unable to locate the document. Next, the researcher contacts the document delivery service. These days that generally means via the World Wide Web, but it could be via fax, a phone call, or even via regular mail.

After receiving the request, the retrieval service will inform the researcher whether or not it is able to provide the requested document, at what cost, in what form, and within what time period. If the researcher is accessing the service via the Web, this information may be returned immediately.

It must here be noted that document delivery services charge for their services. Some require a prepaid subscription for the user even to be able to access their services. While some services may not require a prepaid subscription, such a subscription may allow the user to retrieve documents at a discount from the price paid by the general public. A researcher should inquire at his or her local library if such an arrangement exists.

Other services require no such prepaid arrangement and are able to provide documents on demand to the individual user. Such an arrangement is useful to the occasional user who may request only one or two documents at a time. Payment is generally made online via a credit card. Many of the services provide secure sites for the sending of such sensitive information. It must be noted, however, that transactions in some countries or transactions between countries may not be totally secure. Some services will allow a user to enter all the citation information directly via the Web while they provide a phone number (sometimes toll-free) for the user who does not want to provide credit card information online.

The cost of a document may vary, and is comprised of the copyright fee that the user must pay in order to use this document plus what the retrieval service charges for its services, and sometimes a copying fee based on the number of pages. The fee per document may vary depending on several factors including the length of the document, the cost of the copyright fee, and the method of delivery. Two different delivery services may charge vastly different prices for the same document.

While requesting the document, the user will indicate a preferred method of delivery. Some documents that exist in electronic format may be accessed directly online once the fee is paid and may sometimes be printed directly from there if desired. Or documents may be sent via regular mail, e-mail, or fax. If the requested document exists only in paper format, the fee sometimes pays for converting that document to electronic format so that the user can access it directly over the Web after it has been converted.

The document delivery market is currently undergoing major transition, and the user is cautioned to do diligent research into which may be the best service to use. Bear in mind, of course, that it may be desirable to use more than a single source from time to time.

A list of document delivery providers is given in the appendix, with the caution that things are changing rapidly in this field and any company listed may have been sold or dismantled after press time.

Current Awareness Services

There are services that scholars can use to maintain constant awareness of what is being newly published in their field or areas of interest. These services, often called "current awareness services" or "selective dissemination of information (SDI)," periodically provide to the researcher a report on what has been newly published on specific topics. Most of them function in this way:

The scholar locates a supplier, tells the supplier what his areas of interest are, how often he needs to receive the information (daily, weekly, etc.), and how much information he needs to receive (table of contents, article citations, abstracts, etc.) and contracts with the supplier. The price for the service may be based on some combination of the frequency of updates, the type of information supplied, and the amount of information supplied. While this can be an expensive option, it is an excellent way for the researcher to stay at the forefront of his field.

Untested Resources

There are literally hundreds of millions of documents and information sources available via the Internet and the World Wide Web. Availability does not equal accountability.

Many of the sources are created by people with little knowledge of their topic or with a particular vendetta or an axe to grind. Some of this information is provided by undergraduate students who are just beginning to study in their fields, or even by high school students and younger—often without any indication of who the author is or what his particular level of expertise is in this topic area. Check to determine the date of the information provided; accurate information is often rendered useless by the passage of time. And if possible, try to ascertain whether the information will be available into the future; as noted previously, resources produced by students or by a particular class often disappear or become static when those students move on.

The diligent researcher will examine his sources carefully (whether electronic or otherwise) and apply to them the same criteria used in determining the validity of any reference source.

Free Databases

Some individuals or organizations have mounted databases on the Web that are searchable by anyone at no charge. Some of these databases are limited to a type of media, such as:

- **The CD Database (CDDB)** **<http://www.cddb.com/>**, searchable by artist, album title or song title;

- **The Internet Movie Database** **<http://www.imdb.com/>**, searchable by film title or names of members of the cast and crew.

As always, examine the source in order to evaluate the validity of the information.

Electronic Mailing Lists and Discussion Groups

Mailing lists and discussion groups are like the town square of the Internet: Anyone with an idea, opinion, advice, thought, etc., is allowed to voice it. Anyone else is allowed to agree or disagree. There are lists and groups on every topic imaginable and some that most of us would never imagine! Essentially, this is how they function:

The interested person locates a discussion group, mailing list, or newsgroup of interest and then electronically subscribes. Mailing lists and newsgroups are technologically slightly different; the main difference is that with a mailing list, a copy of every post lands in the subscriber's mailbox and stays there until it is deleted, while newsgroup postings are available for a time and then disappear whether one acts upon them or not. Some newsgroups may simply be viewed without actually subscribing.

Whenever someone has a question or something to share, he or she sends a message to the address of the group. Everyone in the group receives a copy of that message. All responses (except those that are purposely directed to an individual) go to the entire group. The group member can either participate in the discussion or simply view it (called "lurking").

A list of lists can be found at **http://www.liszt.com/**. Liszt is a search engine where one can search for lists on the topic(s) of choice. A search for religion yielded thirty-two categories, each with many lists. A search for lists dealing with "Bible" turned up fifty-nine matches. A search for "theology" gave us fifteen lists.

The information given about each list includes:

- The list name

- The name of the computer that hosts the list

- The name of the contact person(s)

- A description of the list

- Where to get more info

- How to subscribe and unsubscribe

A few newsgroups of possible interest to the researcher in religion and theology are:

- alt.christnet

- alt.christnet.bible

- alt.religion.christian

- soc.religion.christian

The archives of many discussion groups can be found at **http://www.deja.com/**. Because newsgroups are resource-intensive, requiring vast amounts of storage space, and because some are quite controversial,[7] not all newsgroups are carried by every Internet provider. "Although most newsgroups cater to aboveboard hobbies, there's a share of pornographic, incendiary, provocative, and plain moronic material."[8] Some providers may carry all groups, some may carry only select groups and others may carry none at all. The researcher should ask his provider if access to newsgroups is available and how.

Web Rings

Web rings are in a category that falls somewhere between the reliable and the untested sources, as there may be Web rings of both types. A Web ring is simply a consortium of independently mounted sites with pointers to each other. The ring may simply come into existence spontaneously as people with a common interest share resources, may be semi-organized as participants request that each site comply with specific guidelines, or be formally organized with adherence to specific behaviors being part of the price of joining. The latter may be monitored for reliability and conformity. Unfortunately, the scholar often has nothing other than the word of the sites themselves to vouch for their validity.

In a Web ring, each site may point to all other sites, or they may be organized rotationally—that is, site one points to site two, site two points to site three, etc., with the last site pointing back to the first. Web rings can provide pointers to Web sites, particularly smaller ones, which may not have been indexed by the major search engines.

Because Web rings are often mounted by hobbyists, scholars, or those with a particular common interest, they are good places to locate information that is not found elsewhere because it is too esoteric or of limited interest. Because of the interest of the participants in their topic, these sites may provide a depth and breadth of information not available elsewhere. The scholar needs to investigate judiciously the source of the information and determine its reliability before depending on it.

If the search terms one would use to locate a specific topic are too generic or have multiple meanings, a Web ring may be the best starting place for locating other similar sites. The key is locating the first site in the ring—an often difficult task. The best starting place may be one of the general search engines or a college or university site offering studies in that particular subject area.

A good starting point is **WebRing**, variously listed as **http://www.webring.com/**, **http://www.webring.org/**, and **http://www.webring.net/** (All roads lead to Rome). A less well-organized site but interesting for browsing is **The Rail** at **http://www.therail.com/**.

Community Networks

Community networks are another category that falls between reliable and untested resources, depending upon the source of the information contained therein. A single network may contain information running the gamut from very reliable to totally discreditable.

"Community" bears a variety of definitions, ranging from one city or town only to countywide or region-wide. These networks are electronic networks, usually consisting of a series of Web pages pointing to various resources of information on the local community.

Such resources might include information on the area, its businesses, libraries, and community groups, and other resources such as chat rooms or mailing lists. As might be expected, much of the information is of great local interest or of interest to someone studying that particular area.

If one knows where a resource (such as a college or university library) is located geographically but does not know its Web address, one might be able to locate the electronic resource via the network of the community where the institution is located.

One of the first community networks in the United States was the **Michiana Free-Net <http://michiana.org/>**. Other well-known examples are **Chicago Mosaic <http://www.ci.chi.il.us/>**; **San Diego Source <http://www.sddt.com/>**; and **Austin Free-Net <http://www. austinfree.net/>**.

Citing Electronic Resources

Because electronic resources are in a different format than print resources and because they tend to appear and disappear quickly, they require a different form of bibliographic entry. Some of the standard bibliographic guides, such as the *MLA Style Guide*, now devote a section to or have a separate guide on citing electronic resources, and some new guides specifically for citing electronic information have appeared. Sample guides are listed in the bibliography.

Endnotes

1. Lawrence, S.R. and C. L. Giles. "Searching the World Wide Web." *Science* 280 (1998): 98-100.
2. An algorithm is a set of criteria that a search engine uses to automatically analyze a document to determine whether it is appropriate to the information being requested.
3. **http://www.devsearch.com/**. April 1, 2000.
4. As an example of how quickly things change, the exact same search was performed a few minutes later, resulting in 2,252,820 documents. A few weeks later, it yielded 2,415,580 Web pages.
5. Hock, Randolph. *The Extreme Searcher's Guide to Web Search Engines*. Medford, NJ: CyberAge Books, 1999.
6. "Hypertext" or "hyperlinks" are electronic links from the document currently being viewed by the reader to further information. Hyperlinks are usually readily visible within the text. The current convention is for a hyperlink to be blue and underlined, though this is not universally followed. By clicking on the link with the mouse, the user is transferred directly to the information being referred to. The user is cautioned that after connecting to a hyperlink, he may no longer be viewing a document created or maintained by the creator of the original document, and the information contained therein may or may not be reliable.
7. One well known characteristic of newsgroups is that there is at least one group to offend everybody.
8. Kennedy, Angus J. *The Internet: The Rough Guide*. London: Rough Guides Ltd., 1998, p. 129.

Chapter Six

The Research Paper—Putting It All Together

It has been said that the only good research paper is the written research paper. No matter how well the research has been executed or how many resources have been found and examined or how profound the insight into the subject as a result of a vigorous effort in the university library, it is to no avail until the research is written up in a coherent form.

This follow-through, the putting it all together, is what we wish to address ourselves to in this chapter. Our treatment will be brief; it will be simple, but hopefully not simplistic. If the researcher needs more guidance than is offered here, it is available—from the professor, from the library staff, from well-written guides developed for that purpose. Substantial and detailed guides for paper writing may be purchased in the bookstores of most universities, and the better ones are also found in most libraries. But for our purposes here, what follows is what we think to be a sufficient guide for the researcher in the development of an above average research paper or project.

Essentially, two procedures are necessary in order to bring a good paper to fruition, namely, a sound search strategy for the gathering of pertinent information, and then a well-developed organizational framework for the actual writing of the paper. Let us examine this process carefully.

Search Strategy

The search strategy is a prerequisite to all research paper projects. The search strategy model is illustrated in the diagram provided in Figure 6.1 on page 70.

In order for a researcher to write a research paper, he or she must develop a topic that derives from a subject area. Eventually, a well-thought out topic will produce a descriptive title for the actual paper. For the student of religion (or any student or researcher for that matter), an immediate perusal of the background sources constitutes the first step.

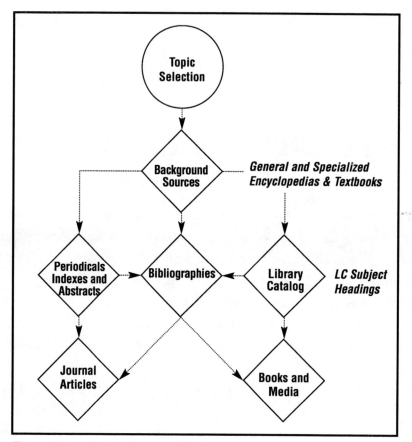

Figure 6.1   Search Strategy Model

The background sources are those general and specialized encyclopedias cited earlier—as well as the textbook if the research is being conducted for a course. (Students often fail to think of the required text in the course as a reference, but it most certainly is.) Another, and probably more effective and time-saving, method for the student of religion and theology would be to go immediately to the twelve-volume *Encyclopedia of Religion and Ethics (ERE),* or the fifteen-volume *New Schaff-Herzog Encyclopedia of Religious Knowledge (SHERK)* that is found in the reference section of most any college or university library. If you are still undecided as to your topic of research, take a volume—any volume—and thumb through it. The titles of areas of theological research jump out at the reader; there are literally hundreds of possibilities, and eventually there will be a subject that even the most unanimated researcher will find interesting.

Read through the article. It will probably be short and written by one of the best minds in the field. If it holds your attention, then either make a photocopy of the bibliography at the end of the article, or copy the entire article. Make sure to write on the first page the entire bibliographical reference, namely: essay author, title of the article, volume, page numbers, and date and place of publication.

Now, after you have first consulted the background sources and identified a subject area (still far removed from the final topic and title of the research paper itself, but certainly a start in the right direction), proceed to the second level of research, namely, the movement from the identification of a subject area to the development of a topic of research.

Topic Development

There are three components of this topic development area. The researcher will consult three very different, but related, areas of information identification.

First Step

First, consult the periodicals indexes and abstracts, and direct special interest and attention toward the *Religion Index One (RIO)* (and book review indexes where applicable). In these sources, you should look up articles in each of several volumes, usually beginning with the most recent volume and working backwards until a substantial amount of literature has been identified. This will vary depending on the area and the topic being pursued, of course.

You should certainly identify two dozen or more articles in the *Religion Index One*, checking the periodicals holdings list to make sure that the articles that are included in the developing bibliography for the research paper are actually available in the library. (If they are not, and if there is sufficient time, the researcher can always call for these articles through the interlibrary loan department or turn to a document delivery service.) The subject area chosen while perusing the *ERE* or *SHERK* should be identified by one, two, or three words, called "key word indicators." These words should be looked up in *Religion Index One.* For example, such key words might be "reformation," "charismatic movement," "fundamentalism," etc.

Second Step

The next step in the search strategy is to consult *Bibliographic Index* and look up the keyword indicators to see if there is already a well-developed and reasonably recent bibliography on the subject area that you are interested in pursuing. If so, much of your work has already been done, for the development of an effective bibliography constitutes a major component in any research effort.

Finally, after gathering a couple of dozen articles from *Religion Index One* (making sure to get complete bibliographic information and not using any abbreviations but writing out every word completely to avoid possible confusion later on), go to the library catalog and look up the key words for a listing of books and related materials held in the library stacks.

Before proceeding to the third step in this search strategy model, we feel compelled to say more about the notes being taken at this point. You are not yet taking notes on the research topic since it is not yet well developed. However, you should be armed with a stack of 3" x 5" or 4" x 6" cards upon which each bibliographic reference is written— one reference per card only. The complete bibliographic notation should include author, title, periodical, volume, issue number, date, pages, as well as the source of the reference, in this instance, *Religion Index One*, and indicating which volume and page number. If you do not take down this information in its entirety more than likely much time will be taken up in wasted steps retracing search procedures and countless hours spent re-doing what should have been done correctly in the first place.

It is a good idea to have a standard form on which to record the needed information. Figure 6.2 provides a suggested format for such a card. You may wish to duplicate a number of these cards ahead of time and then when a reference is found, just fill in the information, remembering to avoid abbreviations.

Author(s)				
Title of Article				
Journal title				
Vol.	No.	Month	Year	Pages
Place of Publication, publisher, date, edition (books only)				
Library where info is located			Call #	
Source of Citation				
How item relates to research problem				
Use reverse side for additional comment. (If used, check here) ☐				

Figure 6.2   Bibliographic Note Card

This point about not abbreviating is being belabored here for a purpose. For example, if you locate in the *RIO* a reference to a splendid article in *ChrTo*, and record the reference as such, by the time you get ready to locate the journal, you may have forgotten the exact and complete title of that specific reference. Then what? Probably a retracing of the reference by means of returning to the *RIO* and checking the reference index to find out that *ChrTo* is *Christianity Today*. If the full title had been recorded the first time, no retracing would need to be done, resulting in time saved.

In the front of almost all reference indexes, in this instance, *Religion Index One*, there is a key to the abbreviations used in the body of the index, which you may refer to if you are in doubt about the correct and full title of certain periodicals. Remember that your note-cards will later serve as the master bibliographic file when you are writing the actual paper. If you make them complete from the outset they will constitute a major help in subsequent writing.

Third Step

This step in the search strategy model is actually using the sources of information, namely, the periodicals and the books identified in the preceding step. The books can be taken out of the library (unless they are categorized as rare books or reference works). The periodical literature often may not be. However, most libraries have copying facilities at minimal cost. Researchers are wise to copy the major articles to be used in their research, thus allowing them to move about with their research portfolio. Otherwise, the note-taking step must occur within the confines of the library, probably in the bound periodicals room. Likewise, articles in electronic format should be printed or saved to disk.

The search has ended. The materials have been identified. This process, once rehearsed, can be executed in an hour or so. A researcher who has been trained in this system of library usage skills can enter the library without any notion of a topic and in less than an hour develop a respectable working bibliography.

From Chaos to Order: The Organizational Framework

At this juncture, you must begin to concentrate seriously upon the organizational model of the research. By now you have moved from no subject area to the discovery, thanks to the *ERE* or *SHERK*, of a viable and interesting subject area.

Furthermore, you have developed the subject area—owing to the three-fold utilization of the search strategy model with **RIO**, **Bibliographic Index**, and the library catalog—into an identifiable topic, and have a working bibliography to prove it. Now you must become acquainted with the materials identified, gleaned, and collected appropriate to the topic.

The following section is a simple, yet workable, process for putting together a research project.

Knowing and Owning the Materials

1. Quick Perusal

Quickly review all the materials you have gathered—two dozen articles or so plus a particularly appropriate book or two on the topic. (Articles, not books, constitute the substance of library research in religion and theology.) If you have photocopies of the articles, discreetly highlight and mark them at particularly important points. The idea here is a general acquaintance with the materials.

2. Outline Development

Develop an outline. Most research papers at this level will have three to five major components with three or four subheadings under each of those. Without an outline, the paper can hardly have a sense of developed logic and reasoned organization to it. The all-too-common practice of writing the outline after the paper has already been written is like drawing up architectural plans for a house already constructed. The purpose of the outline is to help the writer develop the topic.

3. Read Carefully

Following the development of the outline (based on your knowledge of the materials gained in Section 1) with a second and more careful reading of the collected materials is a must. Here, you should be armed with a good supply of note cards. At each opportunity, when you identify something of noteworthy importance to the topic at hand, it should be written down. One quotation or one notation per card—never two or more! This is the wisest rule to follow because later the researcher who has recorded two or three important quotations on a single card may find that one quotation will go in one stack for one point and another quotation (from the same card) will need to go in another stack for a different point. One note per card is imperative.

Furthermore, on each card indicate in the top left-hand corner the author, short-word title of the article, and page number. If this information is not written down on each card as the note is being taken then the chances of the card getting mixed up are overwhelming. When the cards are mixed inadvertently, no matter how excellent the information, if the researcher has no idea of the source of the note or the quotation, this particular card is rendered invalid.

4. Revise and Expand

After you have gleaned all the notes and quotations from the materials gathered for the project, the outline developed in Section 2 must be revised and expanded to incorporate every aspect of the research materials that you wish to include. This usually means: (1) a minor rewording and/or reworking of the major headings and subheadings; and (2) the further development of subheadings, which will provide a means of incorporating most of the notes and quotations taken in Section 3.

5. Cards and Outline

This next to the last step is crucial. Take the outline in its final developed form and place the stack of note cards beside the outline. Holding the stack of cards, label each card in the upper right hand corner (remember the author/short title/page number is in the upper left hand corner) with a Roman numeral corresponding to the major headings of the outline, that is, I, II, III, IV, V, etc. You need to go through the entire stack of cards, labeling them with a major heading number and placing each in its appropriate stack.

Now you will have three or four or five large separate stacks of research cards. That task being accomplished, take stack I (the first major division within the outline) and, proceeding through just that stack alone, mark each card with a subheading A, B, C, D, E, etc., corresponding to the subheadings in the outline under Roman numeral I.

After completing the labeling of the first stack with the subheading letters, proceed to the second and subsequent stacks until all major heading stacks have been divided into the subheading stacks.

Finally, assuming that you have wisely developed sub-subheadings, the cards in the subheadings should be divided into sub-subheading stacks. (This third level indicates excellence in organization with the sub-subheadings often corresponding to individual paragraphs within the finished paper.) That being done, you now have all cards categorized into their appropriate place within the paper. For example, if your paper has three major components I, II, and III, and each of these has three subheadings A, B, C, and each of these has three sub-subheadings 1, 2, 3, then you will have divided the research cards first into three stacks corresponding to I, II, III, and then into nine stacks corresponding to I.A, I.B, I.C, II.A, II.B, II.C, III.A, III.B, and III.C. Finally, you will then sub-divide these nine stacks into three stacks each corresponding to I.A.l, I.A.2, I.A.3, I.B.l, I.B.2, I.B.3, etc. The smaller the stack, the smaller the category of treatment, thereby making the paper develop in its writing in small careful steps versus wild sporadic ones, undisciplined by an outline and organized notecards. (The reason for placing only one bit of information on a single card and identifying that card with author/title/page now becomes apparent.)

6. Number the Cards

Now, turn the cards over and number them consecutively from the first to the very last card. Since they are in exactly the proper order for the writing, this precautionary measure is strictly protective. Now if they are dropped on the floor or mixed up, they can easily and quickly be put back into their proper sequencing.

7. Write the Paper

This, of course, is the whole purpose of the exercise. Line the cards up consecutively beginning with number one and put the information from each card, whether note or quotation, into a coherent style of writing, quoting where needed and paraphrasing otherwise. In no time at all the paper is completed and a successful research project brought to completion.

Chapter Seven

A Review of the Process

Like sports, music, art, or any other skill, research and writing are talents that must be developed. The steps outlined here are just the beginning and give only a few of many possible techniques. But, by following these recommendations, the researcher can work toward developing the process that best meets his needs.

We have suggested the following steps:

The first step—for those with access to a library—is to become acquainted with the facility well in advance of beginning your research. Get to know its collection, its catalog, its layout, and its staff. This process will save many steps and much valuable time when writing under the pressure of a deadline that often accompanies a research project.

Next, learn how to most effectively use the library catalog and to read and interpret individual catalog records. Each entry in the catalog, whether in paper or online, can be a valuable link to many pieces of information on similar topics. Expert researchers make it a priority to master the library catalog, as they understand that it is a vital information tool.

Learn to use the library's reference collection. Public libraries and academic libraries have different foci, and their reference collections will differ accordingly. While a library specializing in the researcher's subject area will be most valuable, there are resources within any library that can be of great benefit if the researcher will take the time to learn how to properly use the available materials.

Remember that the best and most current research is usually based on the most recent information, which is found in the body of periodical literature, particularly the professional journals. In recent times, this body of literature has expanded to include electronic sources as well as print. Both types should be used.

Today's researcher must learn to use the Internet and the many doors it opens, being especially careful to apply good judgment to the validity of sources. While much misinformation and even disinformation appears in print, there is much more of this type of material readily available in the mostly uncontrolled world of the Internet and the

World Wide Web. Used properly, the electronic media can not only lead the researcher to many valuable sources of information but may also actually provide the information itself. Combining the use of the Net and the Web with a good document delivery service gives today's researcher more information than has been available to any previous generation—and more quickly.

Always find the best and most appropriate information. Don't be locked into thinking that the best source is always in print or is always electronic. Either type of source can be good or bad, depending upon the information itself and the qualifications of its creator and the needs of the researcher.

Once the information has been gathered, it is the responsibility of the researcher to manage and manipulate that information into a coherent and logical form that supports his thesis. The technique described in Chapter Six is only one of many. The researcher should take bits and pieces from as many techniques as he has available and mold them into whatever technique works best.

Find the research and writing techniques that work best for you. No one technique will meet the needs of every researcher, nor will a single technique always meet the needs of a given researcher. The more time you spend researching and writing, the better you will become at the process.

In this book, we have given you only the basics and a few research techniques; however, by following these suggestions, you can put together a research project of good quality. By building upon this foundation, you can become a skilled researcher.

Appendix: Resources

Atlases

Aharon, Yohanan and Michael Avi-Yonah. *The Macmillan Bible Atlas*. Completely revised 3rd edition. New York: Macmillan, 1993. 215 pp.

Kraeling, Emil Gottlieb Heinrich. *Rand McNally Bible Atlas*. 3rd edition. Chicago: Rand McNally, 1966. 487 pp.

May, Herbert G., ed. *Oxford Bible Atlas*. 3rd revised edition. New York: Oxford University Press, 1984. 144 pp.

Wright, George Ernest and Floyd Vivian Filson. *The Westminster Historical Atlas to the Bible*. Revised edition. Philadelphia: Westminster, 1956. 130 pp.

Commentaries

Anchor Bible. 2nd edition. Garden City, NY: Doubleday, 1964.

Broadman Bible Commentary. Edited by Clifton J. Allen. Nashville, TN: Broadman Press, 1969-1972. 12 volumes.

A Catholic Commentary on Holy Scripture. Edited by Dom Bernard Orchard, Edmund F. Sutcliffe, Reginald C. Faller, and Dom Ralph Russell. New York: Thomas Nelson and Sons, 1953.

Commentary Practical and Explanatory on the Whole Bible. New edition. Edited by R. Jamieson, A. R. Fansset, & D. Brown. Grand Rapids, MI: Zondervan, 1976.

The International Critical Commentary. Edited by J.A. Emerton and C. E. B. Cranfield. Edinburgh: T. and T. Clark, Ltd., 1982. 20 volumes.

International Critical Commentary on the Holy Scriptures. Edited by Samuel Rolles Driver, Alfred Plummer, and Charles Augustus Briggs. New York: Scribner, 1896-1937. 45 volumes.

The Interpreter's Bible. Edited by George Arthur Buttrick. Nashville, TN: Abingdon, 1984. 12 volumes. Vol. 1: *General Articles, Genesis, Exodus*. 1952 – Vol. 2: *Leviticus—Samuel*. 1953. –Vol. 3: *Kings—Job*. 1954. – Vol. 4: *Psalms, Proverbs*. 1955. – Vol. 5: *Ecclesiastes—Jeremiah*. 1956. – Vol. 6: *Lamentations—Malachi*. 1956. – Vol. 7: *General Articles, Matthew, Mark*. 1951. Vol. 8: *Luke, John*. 1952. – Vol. 9: *The Acts, Romans*. 1954. – Vol. 10: *Corinthians, Ephesians*. 1953. – Vol. 11: *Philippians—Hebrews*. 1955. – Vol.12: *James—Revelation*. 1957.

Interpreter's One-Volume Commentary on the Bible. Edited by Charles M. Laymon. Nashville, TN: Abingdon, 1971. 1386 pp.

Jerome Biblical Commentary. Compiled by Raymond Edward Brown, Joseph A. Fitzmyer, and Roland Edmund Murphy. Englewood Cliffs, NJ: Prentice-Hall, 1980. 2 volumes in one.

New Bible Commentary. 3rd edition, revised. Edited by Donald Guthrie and J. A. Motyer. Grand Rapids, MI: Eerdmans, 1991. 1310 pp. (previously published as Eerdmans' Bible Commentary).

New International Greek Testament Commentary. Edited by W. Ward Gasgne and I. Howard Marshall. Grand Rapids, MI: Wm. B. Eerdmans, 1982. 18 volumes.

The New Jerome Biblical Commentary. Englewood Cliffs, NJ: Prentice-Hall, 1990. 1484 pp.

Peake's Commentary on the Bible. Edited by Matthew Black. New York: Routledge, 1990. 1126 pp.

Dictionaries

Abingdon Dictionary of Living Religions. Edited by Keith Crim. Nashville, TN: Abingdon, 1981. 830 pp.

Attwater, Donald. *The Penguin Dictionary of Saints*. 3rd edition, revised and updated by Catherine Rachel John. New York: Penguin, 1995. 381 pp.

Baring-Gould, Sabine. *The Lives of the Saints, with Introduction and Additional Lives of English Martyrs, Cornish, Scottish, and Welsh Saints, and a full index to the Entire Work*. Revised edition. Edinburgh: Grant, 1993. 16 volumes.

Butler's Lives of the Saints. New full ed./revised by John Cumming. Collegeville, MN: Liturgical Press, 1998. 336 pp.

Concise Oxford Dictionary of the Christian Church. Edited by Elizabeth A. Livingston. 2nd abridged edition. New York: Oxford University Press, 1990. 570 pp.

Dictionary of Hymnology Setting Forth the Origin and History of Christian Hymns of All Ages and Nations. Revised edition. Grand Rapids, MI: Kregel, 1985. 2 volumes.

Dictionary of Pentecostal and Charismatic Movements. 6th printing with corrections. Edited by Stanley M. Burgess and Gary B. McGee. Grand Rapids, MI: Zondervan, 1988. 914 pp.

Farmer, David Hugh. *The Oxford Dictionary of Saints.* 3rd edition. Oxford: Clarendon Press, 1992. 530 pp.

Hastings, James. *Dictionary of the Bible, Dealing with Its Language, Literature and Contents, Including the Biblical Theology.* New York: Scribner, 1898-1904. 5 volumes.

The Interpreter's Dictionary of the Bible; An Illustrated Encyclopedia Identifying and Explaining All Proper Names and Significant Terms and Subjects in the Holy Scriptures, Including the Apocrypha, with Attention to Archaeological Discoveries and Researches into the Life and Faith of Ancient Times. Edited by George Arthur Buttrick. Nashville, TN: Abingdon Press, 1985. 5 volumes.

Moyer, Elgin Sylvester. *Wycliffe Biographical Dictionary of the Church.* Revised and enlarged by Earle E. Cairnes. Chicago: Moody Press, 1982. 449 pp.

The Oxford Dictionary of the Christian Church. Edited by F. L. Cross. 3rd ed., reprinted with corrections edited by E.A. Livingstone. New York: Oxford University Press, 1998. 1786 pp.

Parrinder, Edward Geoffrey. *Dictionary of Non-Christian Religions.* 2nd edition. Amersham, Bucks, Hulton, 1981. 320 pp.

Penguin Dictionary of Religions. Edited by John R. Hinnells. New York: Penguin Books: 1997. 760 pages.

The Perennial Dictionary of World Religions. San Francisco: Harper & Row, 1989. 830 pp. (Originally published under title: *Abingdon Dictionary of Living Religions.* Nashville: Abingdon, 1981.)

Theological Dictionary of the New Testament. Edited by Gerhard Kittel and Gerhard Friedrich. Grand Rapids, MI: William B. Eerdmans, 1985. 10 volumes.

Theological Dictionary of the Old Testament. Revised edition. Edited by C. Johannes Botterweck & Helmer Ringgren. Grand Rapids, MI: Eerdmans, 1997. 5 volumes.

Westminster Dictionary of Church History. Edited by Jerald C. Brauer. Philadelphia: Westminster Press, 1971. 887 pp.

World Christian Encyclopedia: A Comparative Study of Churches and Religions in the Modern World, A.D. 1900-2000. Edited by David B. Barrett. Oxford: Oxford University Press, 1982. 1010 pp.

Wycliffe Bible Encyclopedia. Edited by Charles F. Pfeiffer, Howard F. Vox and John Rea. Chicago: Moody Press, 1983. 2 volumes.

Document Delivery Suppliers
Specialized

Business
Technical Information Service
http://thorplus.lib.purdue.edu/tis/powerize.com

Business Research Center
http://www.infoMarket.k-link.com/

FIND/SVP: Business Research, Consulting and Management Advisory Services
http://www.findsvp.com/

HBS Publishing: Harvard Business Review
http://www.hbsp.harvard.edu/products/hbr/index.html

Capitol District Information, Inc. (CDI)
http://www.capitoldistrict.com/

Chemistry
ChemPort
http://www.chemport.org/

ChemWeb
http://www.ChemWeb.com/

Computing
ACM: Digital Library
http://www.acm.org/dl/

Dissertations
UMI ProQuest Digital Dissertations
http://wwwlib.umi.com/dissertations/

UMI: Online Dissertation Services
http://www.umi.com/hp/Products/Dissertations.html

Dissertation Express
http://www.umi.com/hp/Products/DisExpress.html

Legal
Research Associates
http://www.researchassociates.net/

Newspapers
NewsLibrary Search
http://www.newslibrary.com/

NewsDirectory.com
http://www.newsdirectory.com

Patents
Polyresearch Service/Patent information services & searches
http://www.polyresearch.com/

Science
ISI Document Solution:Institute for Scientific Information
http://www.isinet.com/prodserv/ids/idsprod.html

Technical Information Service
http://thorplus.lib.purdue.edu/tis/

HighWire Press
http://highwire.stanford.edu/

Bioline Publications
http://www.bdt.org.br/bioline/

Buy An Article
http://ojps.aip.org/jhtml/artinphys/aipmain.html

BioMedNet
http://www.biomednet.com/

Technology
Technical Information Service
http://thorplus.lib.purdue.edu/tis/

General

Uncover Reveal
http://uncweb.carl.org:80/reveal/

UnCoverWeb
http://uncweb.carl.org/

UnCover SOS Service
http://uncweb.carl.org/sos/sosform.html

UMI: The Digital Vault Initiative
http://www.umi.com/hp/Features/DVault/

Teldan Information Systems Ltd
http://www.teldan.co.il/docdeliv.html

TDI Library Services, Inc.
http://tdico.com/home.html

OPAC 97
http://opac97.bl.uk/

Northern Light Search
http://www.northernlight.com/search.html

Infotrieve Online
http://www3.infotrieve.com/

InformationQuest
http://www.eiq.com/

Information Resource Services, Inc.
http://www.librarianoncall.com/

Information Prime NA, Inc.
http://www.infoprime.com/index.htm

Infocus Research Services
http://www.infocus-research.com/

New York Public Library Research Libraries
http://www.nypl.org/research/docdelivery/index.html

Electric Library Personal Edition
http://www.elibrary.com/

ASM International
http://www.asm-intl.org/www-asm/library/docdel.htm

F.Y.I.—County of Los Angeles Public Library
http://www.colapublib.org/fyi/city/doc_del/index.html

The Research Investment, Inc.
http://www.researchinvest.com/tridoc.html

Doc Deliver
http://www.docdeliver.com/

Carolina Library Services
http://www.intrex.net/carolib/default.htm

Cal Info
http://members.aol.com/calinfola/retrieve.htm

Cadence Group
http://www.cadence-group.com/

Kessler-Hancock
http://www.khinfo.com/

The British Library
http://www.bl.uk/

Advanced Information Consultants
http://advinfoc.com/

U. of Washington Libraries Research Express
http://www.lib.washington.edu/Resxp/docdel.com
http://www.docdel.com/

Outside the U.S

HighWire Press
http://intl.highwire.org/

Asia
Japan
JICST Library Document Delivery Service
http://www.jst.go.jp/EN/JICST/ServiceGuide/ext-serv.html

Infonetwork
http://www.doc-quest.com/

Australia
Business Information Service: State Library of Victoria
http://www.slv.vic.gov.au/slv/business/bis.htm

National Library of Australia Document Supply Service
http://www.nla.gov.au/dss/

MONINFO Home (Monash University)
http://www.lib.monash.edu.au/moninfo/

Rapid Services—UNSW\
http://www.library.unsw.edu.au/rapid.html

Europe
Austria

Central Library for Physics in Vienna
http://www.univie.ac.at/zbph/

Zentralbibliothek für Physik in Wien
http://www.zbp.univie.ac.at/default.htm

England

IEE—The IEE Library—Main services
http://www.iee.org.uk/Library/

London Business School Information Service
http://www.lbs.ac.uk/library/services/general_library_services/document_delivery/document_delivery.html

British Library Document Supply Centre
http://www.bl.uk/services/bsds/dsc/delivery.html

Finland

Helsinki School of Economics Library
http://helecon.hkkk.fi/library/

Germany

DBI-LINK die Verbindung zwischen Benutzer und Bibliothek
http://www.dbilink.de/en/

Document Delivery Service of the Tübingen University Library
http://www.uni-tuebingen.de/ub/ssg-s_.htm

German National Library of Medicine—Cologne
http://www.uni-koeln.de/zentral/zbib-med/index.en.html

The Broker Research Center—Delivery of patent copies
http://www.infobroker.de/service/patdele.html

Ireland

University of Limerick's Business & Technical Information Service
http://www.btis.ie/

Italy

Quaestio-INFORMATION BROKER

http://www.quaestio.it/

Netherlands

AGRALIN home page

http://www.bib.wau.nl/

Polyresearch Service—Patent information services and searches

http://www.polyresearch.com/

The NIWI Web Site

http://www.niwi.knaw.nl/

Inhoud van de NIWI Web Site

http://www.niwi.knaw.nl/nl/homepag.htm

NIWI Web Site [English]

http://www.niwi.knaw.nl/us/homepag.htm

Russia

Access Russia Information Services

http://www.arussia.com/

Russian Periodicals Online

http://www.russianstory.com/

Scotland

Recal Information Services

http://www.recal.org.uk/

Latin America

Argentina

Ontyme Information Brokers

http://www.informar.com.ar/

Middle East

Israel

Infomayda

http://www.actcom.co.il/~atoz/

North America

Canada

Canada Institute for Scientific and Technical Information (CISTI)
http://www.cisti.nrc.ca/cisti/docdel/docdel.html

University of Waterloo Electronic Library Information Services
http://www.lib.uwaterloo.ca/InfoServ.html

Micromedia Limited
http://www.micromedia.on.ca/

Current Awareness Services

Information Express
http://www.express.com/

Encyclopedias

Catholic Encyclopedia; an International Work of Reference on the Constitution, Doctrine, Discipline, and History of the Catholic Church. New York: Encyclopedia Press, 1983.

Encyclopedia Judaica. New York: Macmillan, 1972. 16 volumes.

Encyclopedia of Biblical Theology: The Complete Sacramentum Verbi. Edited by Johannes B. Bauer. New York: Crossroad, 1981. 1141 pp.

Encyclopedia of Religion and Ethics. Edited by James Hastings. New York: Charles Scribner, 1980. 13 volumes.

The Encyclopedia of Philosophy. Edited by Paul Edwards. New York: Simon & Schuster and Prentice Hall International, 1996. 8 volumes.

Encyclopedia of Theology: The Concise Sacramentum Mundi. Edited by Karl Rahner. Tunbridge Wells: Burns & Oates, 1993. 1841 pp.

The International Standard Bible Encyclopedia. Edited by Geoffrey W. Bromiley. Revised edition. Grand Rapids, MI: Eerdmans, 1986. 2 volumes.

The Jewish Encyclopedia. New York: Gordon Press, 1976. 10 volumes.

Melton, J. Gordon. *The Encyclopedia of American Religions.* 6th edition. Detroit: Gale Research, 1999.

New Catholic Encyclopedia. Catholic University of America. Palatine, IL: J. Heraty, 1989. 18 volumes.

The New Schaff-Herzog Encyclopedia of Religious Knowledge Embracing Biblical, Historical, Doctrinal and Practical Theology and Biblical, Theological and Ecclesiastical Biography, from the Earliest Times to the Present Day. Based on the third edition of the *Realencyklopadie* founded by J. J. Herzog and edited by Alber Hauck. Samuel Macauley Jackson, editor-in-chief. Grand Rapids, MI: Baker Book House, 1977. 13 volumes.

New Standard Jewish Encyclopedia. 7th edition. Edited by Geoffrey Wigoder. New York: Facts on File, 1992.

Sacramentum Mundi; An Encyclopedia of Theology. New York: Herder & Herder, 1968-1970. 6 volumes.

Twentieth Century Encyclopedia of Religious Knowledge: An Extension of the New Schaff Herzog Encyclopedia of Religious Knowledge. Edited by Lefferts A. Loetscher. Grand Rapids, MI: Baker Book House, 1970. 2 volumes.

Who's Who in Religion. Chicago: Marquis, 1975–.

Lexicons, Concordances, and Handbooks

American Jewish Year Book. New York: Jewish Publishing Society, 1900–. Annual.

Computer Bible: A Critical Concordance. J. Arthur Baird and David Noel Freedman, editors. Wooster, OH: Biblical Research Associates, 1971–. 25 volumes.

Computer Bible: King James Version. Colorado Springs, CO: Navpress, 1990. 8 computer disks; 5 1/4 in. + user's guide.

Computer Bible: New International Version. Colorado Springs, CO: Navpress, 1990. 8 computer disks; 5 1/4 in. + user's guide.

Cruden, Alexander. *Cruden's Complete Concordance to the Old and New Testaments by Alexander Cruden, A. M.*, edited by A. D. Adams, C. H. Irwin, and S. A. Waters. Grand Rapids, MI: Zondervan, 1968. (This popular title is available in many editions from several publishers.)

Directory of Religious Organizations in the United States. 3rd ed. Detroit: Gale Research Inc., 1993. 728 pp.

A Greek-English Lexicon of the New Testament. Edited by Frederick W Danker and F. Wilber Gingrich; William F. Arndt, translator. Chicago: University of Chicago Press, 1979.

Halley, Henry H. *Halley's Bible Handbook.* 24th edition. Grand Rapids, MI: Zondervan, 1994.

Harvey, Van Austin. *A Handbook of Theological Terms.* First Touchstone edition. New York: Macmillan, 1997. 253 pp.

Mead, Frank Spencer. *Handbook of Denominations in the United States.* New 10th edition, revised by Samuel S. Hill. Nashville, TN: Abingdon, 1985. 352 pp.

Strong, James. *The Strong's New Concordance of the Bible: Popular Edition.* Nashville, TN: Thomas Nelson, 1985. (This popular title is available in many editions from several publishers.)

Yearbook of American and Canadian Churches. Nashville: Abingdon, 1916–. Annual.

Young, Robert. *Young's Analytical Concordance to the Bible.* Peabody, MA: Hendrickson Publishers, 1992.

Other References

Batten, Donna. *Guide to U. S. Government Publications.* Farmiongton Hills, MI: The Gale Group.

The Ante-Nicene Fathers; Translations and Writing of the Fathers Down to A. D. 325. Edited by A. Cleveland Cox. Grand Rapids, MI: William B. Eerdmans, 1989. 10 volumes.

Bruce, F. F. *History of the Bible in English.* 3rd edition. New York: Oxford University Press, 274 pp.

Cambridge History of the Bible. Cambridge University Press, 1963-1970. 3 volumes.

Cambridge History of Judaism. Edited by Louis W. S. Davies and Louis Finkelstein. New York: Cambridge University Press, 1989–. 4 volumes.

Gates, Jean Key. *Guide to the Use of Libraries and Information Sources,* 7th edition. New York: McGraw-Hill, 1994.

History of the Christian Church. Edited by Philip Schaff. 3rd edition. Peabody, MA: Hendrickson Publishers, 1996. 8 volumes. Vol. 1: *Apostolic Christianity.* – Vol. 2: *Ante-Nicene. 100-325.* – Vol. 3: *Nicene & Post-Nicene. 311-600.* – Vol. 4: *Medieval Christianity. 590-1073.* – Vol. 5: *Middle Ages. 1049-1294.* – Vol. 6: *Middle Ages. 1295-1517.* – Vol. 7: *German Reformation.* – Vol. 8: *Swiss Reformation.*

Morehead, Joe. *Introduction to United States Public Documents.* 3rd edition. Littleton, CO: Libraries Unlimited, Inc., 1983. 309 pp.

Nicene and Post-Nicene Fathers, the First Series. Edited by Philip Schaff. Edinburgh: T. & T. Clark, 1986. 14 volumes.

Nicene and Post-Nicene Fathers, the Second Series. Edited by Philip Schaff and Henry Wace. Edinburgh: T. & T. Clark, 1986. 14 volumes.

Oxford History of the Christian Church. New York: Oxford University Press, 1976–.

Religious Books 1876-1982: Subject Index, Author Index, Title Index. New York: Bowker, 1983. 4 volumes.

Sandeen, Ernest Robert and Frederick Hale. *American Religion and Philosophy: A Guide to Information Sources*. Detroit: Gale, 1978. 377 pp. (*American Studies Information Guide Series*, Volume 5).

Schaff, Philip. *History of the Christian Church*. Revised edition. New York: Scribner, 1882-1910. 7 volumes in eight volumes.

Schmeckebier, Laurence F. and Roy Be Eastin. *Government Publications and Their Use*. 2nd revised edition. Washington, DC: The Brookings Institute, 1986. 502 pp.

Stevenson, Burton Egbert. *The Home Book of Bible Quotations*. New York: Harper, 1977. 645 pp.

Indexes

Bibliographic Index. [New York]: H.W. Wilson Co., 1938–.

Biography Index. New York: H.W. Wilson Co., 1946–.

Book Review Digest. New York: H.W. Wilson Company, 1905–.

Book Review Index. Detroit: Gale Research Co., 1965–.

Catholic Periodical and Literature Index. Haverford, PA: Catholic Library Association, 1933–.

Christian Periodical Index. Buffalo, NY: Association of Christian Librarians, 1958–.

Cumulative Book Index. Quarterly. [New York]: H.W. Wilson Co., 1898–.

Current Book Review Citations. New York: H.W. Wilson Co., 1976–1982.

The Guide to Social Science and Religion in Periodical Literature. Flint, MI: National Periodical Library, 1969.

Humanities Index. New York: H.W. Wilson Co., 1974–.

Index to Jewish Periodicals. Cleveland: Index to Jewish Periodicals. 1963–. Semiannual.

Index to U.S. Government Periodicals. [Chicago]: Infordata International, 1970–1987.

INFOTRAC. Foster City, CA: Information Access Co., 1985–.

New Testament Abstracts. Cambridge, MA: Weston School of Theology, 1956–. Three times per year.

Old Testament Abstracts. Washington, DC: Catholic Biblical Association of America, 1978–. Three times per year.

PAIS International (Public Affairs Information Service Bulletin). New York: Public Affairs Information Service, 1915–.

Readers' Guide to Periodical Literature. New York: H.W. Wilson Co., 1901–.

Religion Index One: Periodicals. Chicago: American Theological Libraries Association, 1953–. Semiannual.

Religion Index Two: Multi-Author Works. Chicago: American Theological Libraries Association, 1978–. Annual.

Religious and Theological Abstracts. Myerstown, Pennsylvania: Theological Publishers, 1958–. Quarterly.

Social Sciences Index. New York: H.W. Wilson Co., 1974– .

Major Religion Periodicals

Church History. Berne, IN: American Society of Church History, 1931–.

Dialog: A Journal of Theology. Minneapolis, MN: Sacred Design Associates, 1962–.

History of Religions. [Chicago]: University of Chicago Press, 1961–.

Interpretation: A Journal of Bible and Theology. [Richmond, VA: Union Theological Seminary in Virginia, 1947–.

Journal of Ecumenical Studies. [Philadelphia]: Temple University, 1964–.

Journal of Jewish Studies. [Cambridge, England]: 1948–.

Journal of Religion. [Chicago]: University of Chicago Press, 1921–.

Journal of Religious Ethics. [Waterloo, Ontario]: American Academy of Religion, 1973–.

Journal of Theological Studies. London: New York: Macmillan and Co.; Macmillan Co., 1900–.

Muslim World. [Hartford, Conn.]: Duncan Black Macdonald Center at the Hartford Seminary Foundation, 1911–.

Religious Studies. London; New York: Cambridge University Press, 1965–.

Theological Studies. New York: America Press, 1940–.

Theology Today. Lancaster, PA: Theology Today, 1943–.

Style Sheets for Citing Electronic Information

Gibaldi, Joseph. *MLA Handbook for Writers of Research Papers*, 5th edition. New York: Modern Language Association of America, 1999.

Greenhill, Anita. *Electronic References & Scholarly Citations of Internet Sources*. Queensland: Griffith University, 1995.

Harnack, Andrew. *Beyond the MLA Handbook: Documenting Electronic Sources on the Internet*. Richmond, KY: Eastern Kentucky University, 1999.

Li, Xia, and Nancy Crane. *Electronic Styles: A Handbook for Citing Electronic Information*, 2nd ed. Medford, NJ: Information Today, 1996.

Thibault, Danielle. *Bibliographic Style Manual*. Ottawa: National Library of Canada, 1998.

Walker, Janice R. *The Columbia Guide to Online Style*. New York: Columbia University Press, 1998.

Walker, Janice R. *MLA-Style Citations of Electronic Sources*. Tampa, FL: Janice R. Walker, 1995.

Winkler, Anthony C. *Writing the Research Paper: A Handbook with Both the MLA and APA Documentation Styles*, 5th ed. Fort Worth: Harcourt Brace College Publishers, 1999.

Internet and Online Resources

Bookstores

Amazon.com
http://www.amazon.com/

Barnes and Noble
http://www.barnesandnoble.com/

Bibliofind
http://www.bibliofind.com/

Blackwell's
http://bookshop.blackwells.co.uk/

The Bookpl@ce
http://www.thebookplace.com/

Bookwire
http://www.bookwire.com/

Borders
http://borders.com/

internet bookshop
http://www.bookshop.co.uk/

Project Gutenberg
http://promo.net/pg/

Waterstone's
http://www.waterstones.co.uk/

Community Networks
Michiana Free-Net
http://michiana.org/

Chicago Mosaic
http://www.ci.chi.il.us/

San Diego Source
http://www.sddt.com/

Austin Free-Net
http://www.austinfree.net/

Databases
The Internet Movie Database
http://www.imdb.com/

The CD Database (CDDB)
http://www.cddb.com/

Dictionaries
The LOGOS Dictionary
http://www.logos.it/

OneLook Dictionaries
http://www.onelook.com/

Merriam-Webster
http://www.m-w.com/

Roget's Thesaurus
http://thesaurus.com/

The Semantic Rhyming Dictionary
http://www.link.cs.cmu.edu/dougb/rhyme-doc.html

A Web of On-line Dictionaries
http://www.facstaff.bucknell.edu/rbeard/diction.html

Government Resources

CCTA Information Service
http://www.open.gov.uk/

Federal Information Center (FIC)
http://fic.info.gov/

FedWorld
http://www.fedworld.gov/

Government Information Xchange
http://www.info.gov/cgi-bin/search_gov/

Links for U.S. federal government
http://ecs.rams.com/wwwlinks/listlink.cfm?cat=33

United States Government Printing Office
http://www.gpo.gov/

U.S. Census Bureau
http://www.census.gov/

U.S. Senate
http://www.senate.gov/

U.S. House
http://www.house.gov/

The White House
http://www.whitehouse.gov/

Libraries and Library Networks

ACLIN, Access Colorado Library and Information Network
http://www.aclin.org/

The British Library
http://portico.bl.uk/

Galileo: Georgia Library Learning Online
http://www.galileo.peachnet.edu/

INSPIRE, Indiana Spectrum of Information Resources
http://www.inspire-indiana.net/

Internet Public Library
http://www.ipl.org/

Library of Congress
http://www.loc.gov/

National Library of Canada
http://www.nlc-bnc.ca/

SAILOR, Maryland's Online Public Information Network
http://www.sailor.lib.md.us/

Miscellaneous
Bartlett's Familiar Quotations
http://www.columbia.edu/acis/bartleby/bartlett/

Harvard Business School
http://www.hbs.harvard.edu/

Project Bartleby Archive
http://www.columbia.edu/acis/bartleby/

Newsgroups and Mailing Lists
Dejanews
http://www.dejanews.com/

Liszt
http://www.liszt.com/

Publicly Accessible Mailing Lists
http://www.neosoft.com/internet/paml/

Organizations
American Cancer Society
http://www.cancer.org/

American Heart Association
http://www.americanheart.org

American Medical Association
http://www.ama-assn.org/

American Psychological Association
http://www.apa.org/

Radio and TV Stations

Broadcast.com
http://www.broadcast.com/

Religious Resources

Academic Info Religion: Subject Index
http://www.academicinfo.net/religindex.html

The Anglican Domain
http://www.anglican.org/

The Bible Gateway
http://bible.gospelcom.net/

Catholic Information Network
http://www.cin.org/

Council for Christian Colleges & Universities
http://www.gospelcom.net/cccu/

Gospel Communications Network
http://www.gospelcom.net/

A Guide To Religious Studies Resources On The Internet, John L Gresham, MLS, PhD
http://www.fontbonne.edu/libserv/fgic/fgic.htm

Harvard Divinity School
http://divweb.harvard.edu/

Mission-Related Organizations at Gospelcom
http://www.gospelcom.net/welcome/categories/missions.shtml

Search Engines (General)

About.com
http://www.about.com/

Altavista
http://www.altavista.com/

DirectHit
http://www.directhit.com/

Excite
http://www.excite.com/

Go Network (Formerly InfoSeek)
http://www.infoseek.go.com/

Google
http://www.google.com/

Goto.com
http://www.goto.com/

HotBot
http://www.hotbot.com/

LookSmart
http://www.looksmart.com/

Lycos
http://www.lycos.com/

Magellan
http://www.mckinley.com/

Netscape Search
http://search.netscape.com/

Northern Light
http://www.nlsearch.com/

Snap.com
http://home.snap.com/

Thunderstone
http://www.thunderstone.com/

Webcrawler
http://www.webcrawler.com/

Yahoo!
http://www.yahoo.com/

Search Engines (Specialized)
BusinessWeb
http://www.businesswebsource.com/

DevSearch
http://www.devsearch.com/

Search Engines (Metasearch)

Dogpile
http://www.dogpile.com/

Metacrawler
http://www.metacrawler.com/

Web Rings

Bomis.com
http://www.bomis.com/

The Rail
http://www.therail.com/

WebRing
http://www.webring.com/

About the Author

Dennis C. Tucker is School Library Consultant and Member Liaison at Indiana Cooperative Library Services Authority (INCOLSA) in Indianapolis, Indiana. He has been with INCOLSA since 1990 and has also served as director of *Project Hi-Net*—a two-million-dollar automation grant to the 31 high schools in Indianapolis, which he co-authored—and as Library Automation Consultant. Formerly, he worked at the University of Notre Dame and was Library Director at Bethel College in Mishawaka, Indiana. He has worked as a school librarian and was an officer of the Southeast Missouri Department of School Librarians.

Tucker is a member of the Association of Indiana Media Educators (AIME), the Indiana Library Federation (ILF), the Association of Christian Librarians, Church and Synagogue Library Association, Evangelical Church Library Association, and the American Library Association (ALA). Within ALA, he is a member of the International Relations Round Table Hospitality subcommittee, the Library and Information Technology Association's Regional Institutes Committee, and an External Review Panel participant for the Committee on Accreditation. He currently serves as director-at-large for the Library Automation and Technology Division of the Indiana Library Federation.

He holds an MAT in English from Southeast Missouri State University, an MLS from the University of Missouri-Columbia, and is currently a doctoral candidate in a cooperative program through the Graduate Theological Foundation and the University of Oxford.

Tucker is author of many books, reviews, and articles, including a stint as monthly columnist for *American Libraries*. His most recent monograph is *Library Relocations and Collection Shifts* (Information Today, Inc., 1999). He has also worked as a teacher of Spanish, English, and ESL, and as an instructor in the field of Library Science.

Index

More books of interest from Information Today, Inc.

Introductory Concepts in Information Science

Melanie J. Norton

Melanie J. Norton presents a unique, carefully researched introduction to the practical and theoretical concepts of information science, and examines the impact of the Information Age on society and its institutions. Drawing on recent research into the field, as well as from scholarly and trade publications, this monograph provides a brief history of information science and coverage of key topics, including communications and cognition, information retrieval, bibliometrics, modeling, economics, information policies, and the impact of information technology on modern management. An essential volume for graduate students, practitioners, and professionals who need a solid grounding in the field of information science.

Hardbound • ISBN 1-57387-087-0
ASIS Members $31.60   Non-Members $39.50

Design Wise
A Guide for Evaluating the Interface Design of Information Resources

Alison J. Head

"Design Wise takes us beyond what's cool and what's hot and shows us what works and what doesn't."
—Elizabeth Osder, The New York Times on the Web

Knowing how to size up user-centered interface design is becoming as important for people who choose and use information resources as for those who design them. This book introduces readers to the basics of interface design and explains why a design evaluation should be tied to the use and purchase of information resources.

Softbound • ISBN 0-910965-31-5 • $29.95
Hardbound • ISBN 0-910965-39-0 • $39.95

The Extreme Searcher's Guide to Web Search Engines
A Handbook for the Serious Searcher

Randolph Hock
Foreword by Paula Berinstein

Whether you're a new Web user or an experienced online searcher, here's a practical guide that shows you how to make the most of the leading Internet search tools. Written by leading Internet trainer Randolph (Ran) Hock, this book gives an in-depth view of the major search engines, explaining their respective strengths, weaknesses, and features, and providing detailed instructions on how to use each to its maximum potential. As a reader bonus, the author maintains a regularly-updated Web page that supports the book.

Softbound • ISBN 0-910965-26-9 • $24.95
Hardbound • ISBN 0-910965-38-2 • $34.95

Library Relocations and Collection Shifts

Dennis Tucker

In *Library Relocations and Collection Shifts*, author, librarian, and move director Dennis C. Tucker explains how to develop an appropriate moving plan for a library of any type or size. A thorough revision of his classic, *From Here to There: Moving a Library*, the book provides coverage of all these topics and more:

- Appointing a move director and committee
- Customizing a moving plan for your library
- Handling books and periodicals
- Working with professional movers

- Moving methods and strategies
- Planning and coordinating the move
- Cleaning, fumigation, and deacidification
- Communicating with staff and the public

You'll also find information on using spreadsheets to shift periodical collections, a sample moving contract, a directory of useful resources, and suggestions for further reading.

Hardbound • ISBN 1-57387-069-2 • $35.00

The Evolving Virtual Library II
Practical and Philosophical Perspectives

Edited by Laverna M. Saunders

This new edition of *The Evolving Virtual Library* documents how libraries of all types are changing with the integration of the Internet and the Web, electronic resources, and computer networks. It provides a summary of trends over the last five years, new developments in networking, case studies of creating digital content delivery systems for remote users, applications in K-12 and public libraries, and a vision of things to come. The contributing experts are highly regarded in their specialties. The information is timely and presents a snapshot of what libraries are dealing with in the new millennium.

Topics include:
- Mining the Information Networks: Intranets and Extranets at Work
- Building a Digital Library: The Stories of the Making of America
- A Public Library in Transition: Paradigm Shifts Toward the New Millennium

Hardbound • ISBN 1-57387-070-6 • $39.50

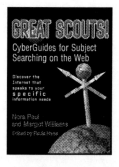

Great Scouts!
CyberGuides for Subject Searching on the Web

Nora Paul and Margot Williams
Edited by Paula Hane • Foreword by Barbara Quint

Great Scouts! is a cure for information overload. Authors Nora Paul (The Poynter Institute) and Margot Williams *(The Washington Post)* direct readers to the very best subject-specific, Web-based information resources. Thirty chapters cover specialized "CyberGuides" selected as the premier Internet sources of information on business, education, religion, arts and entertainment, science and technology, health and medicine, politics and government, law, sports, and much more. With its expert advice and evaluations of information and link content, value, currency, stability, and usability, *Great Scouts!* takes you "beyond search engines"—directly to the top sources of information for your topic. As a reader bonus, the authors are maintaining a Web page featuring updated links to all the sites covered in the book.

Softbound • ISBN 0-910965-27-7 • $24.95

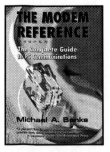

The Modem Reference, 4th Edition
The Complete Guide to PC Communications

Michael A. Banks

"If you can't find the answer to a telecommunications problem here, there probably isn't an answer."
—Lawrence Blasko, The Associated Press

Now in its 4th edition, this popular handbook explains the concepts behind computer data, data encoding, and transmission, providing practical advice for PC users who want to get the most from their online operations. In his uniquely readable style, author and techno-guru Mike Banks *(The Internet Unplugged)* takes readers on a tour of PC data communications technology, explaining how modems, PC fax systems, computer networks, and the Internet work. He provides an in-depth look at how data are communicated between computers all around the world, demystifying the terminology, hardware, and software. *The Modem Reference* is a must-read for students, professional online users, and all computer users who want to maximize their PC fax and data communications capability.

Softbound • ISBN 0-910965-36-6 • $29.95

ARIST 34
Annual Review of Information Science and Technology

Edited by Martha E. Williams

Since 1966, *ARIST* has been continuously at the cutting edge in contributing a useful and comprehensive view of the broad field of information science and technology. *ARIST* reviews numerous topics within the field and ultimately provides this annual source of ideas, trends, and references to the literature. The series encompasses the entire field in all its aspects. Topics for the annual volume are selected on the basis of timeliness and an assessment of reader interest.

Contents of Volume 34 include:

- The History of Documentation and Information Science
- Applications of Machine Learning in Information Retrieval
- Privacy and Digital Information
- Cognitive Information Retrieval
- Text Mining
- Methodologies for Human Behavioral Research
- Measuring the Internet
- Infometric Laws
- Using and Reading Scholarly Literature
- Literature Dynamics: Studies on Growth, Diffusion, and Epidemics

Hardbound • ISBN 1-57387-093-5
ASIS Members $79.95   Non-Members $99.95

Electronic Styles
A Handbook for Citing Electronic Information

Xia Li and Nancy Crane

This second edition of the best-selling guide to referencing electronic information and citing the complete range of electronic formats includes text-based information, electronic journals and discussion lists, Web sites, CD-ROM and multimedia products, and commercial online documents.

Softbound • ISBN 1-57387-027-7 • $19.99

Teaching with Technology
Rethinking Tradition

Edited by Les Lloyd

This latest informative volume from Les Lloyd includes contributions from leading experts on the use of technology in higher education. Four sections are included: Cross-Discipline Use of Technology, The Web as a Tool in Specific Disciplines, Technology Management for Faculty and Administration, and Techniques for Enhancing Teaching in Cross-Discipline Courses. If your college or university needs to be on the cutting edge of the technology revolution, this book is highly recommended.

Hardbound • ISBN 1-57387-068-4 • $39.50

The SOLO Librarian's Sourcebook

Judith A. Siess

A founding force in the formation of the SOLO Librarian's Division of the Special Libraries Association, Judith Siess has written the definitive sourcebook for all librarians who work in one-person libraries in the U.S. and abroad: public, law, museum, corporate, hospital, school, church, and prison. She covers such topics as the solo librarian and management issues, education requirements, technology, outsourcing and downsizing, and the future, as well as providing lists of vendors, schools of education, books and journals, and Internet sites.

Hardbound • ISBN 1-57387-032-3 • $39.50

Internet Blue Pages, 2001-2002 Edition
The Guide to Federal Government Web Sites

Laurie Andriot

With over 1,800 Web addresses, this guide is designed to help you find any agency easily. Arranged in accordance with the US Government Manual, each entry includes the name of the agency, the Web address (URL), a brief description of the agency, and links to the agency's or subagency's home page. For helpful cross-referencing, an alphabetical agency listing and a comprehensive index for subject searching are also included. Regularly updated information and links are provided on the author's Web site.

Softbound • ISBN 0-910965-29-3 • $34.95